0480

Drugs

D0430790

Drugs and Drinking

What Every Teen and Parent Should Know

JAY STRACK

Thomas Nelson Publishers
Nashville • Camden • New York

Eighth printing

Published in Nashville, Tennessee, by Thomas Nelson, Inc. and distributed in Canada by Lawson Falle, Ltd., Cambridge, Ontario.

Printed in the United States of America.

Scripture quotations are from The King James Version of the Bible.

Library of Congress Cataloging in Publication Data

Strack, Jay.
  Drugs and drinking.

  Bibliography: p. 213
  1. Youth—United States—Drug use. 2. Drug abuse—
United States. 3. Drug abuse—United States—
Prevention. 4. Adolescent psychology. I. Title.
HV5824.Y68S84   1985   362.2'93'088055   85-271
ISBN 0-8407-5698-4

To my beloved wife Diane,
who has given me
the greatest years of my life.
She is my partner, my friend, and my helpmate.
For all the sacrifice
and for all the times she understood
when I was gone
trying to rescue teens in trouble,
I thank her.

Contents

Preface

OF ALL THE PROBLEMS OF AMERICAN life today, few are more disturbing to most adults than the problem of drug abuse among the young. As a society, America has always been deeply concerned with her children. Since the beginning of the seventeenth century, foreign observers have remarked about how Americans cherish and yet spoil their children.

Today we have much to be concerned about. Millions of young people are hiding behind a chemical curtain of drugs, and millions more are drowning in a sea of alcohol. Let's face it: If you are a parent with a child between the ages of five and twenty, your child will be exposed to drug abuse through the medicine chest, the school, the hangout, the radio, and the television. America's reliance on drugs is unequaled in the history of mankind. We take pills to pep us up, to calm us down, to gain weight, to lose weight, to avoid conception, and to increase fertility. Drugs are a two-edged sword, capable both of saving lives and of ruining them. Drug abuse poses a major health and social danger.

Drug abuse is nothing new; it has been a problem for years. But ten or twenty years ago it was easier to ignore drug addiction, as well as abortion, illegitimate births, and broken homes, so long as these problems did not affect most of us. Today, however, these problems are spreading at epidemic proportions in middle schools and senior high schools and colleges.

The drug scene has changed somewhat since I wrote this book in 1979. In the 1980s cocaine seems to be replacing heroin, which has been filling hospitals in the past decade. My new material on cocaine, including how to get off it, is of considerable importance. I have also documented the major change in the nature and amount of marijuana being grown and sold. The dangers of marijuana have been grossly underrated by this generation. Drug abuse among young people in the United States has reached bewildering proportions. Twenty percent of youths twelve to seventeen years old claimed use of at least one drug (excluding cigarettes and alcohol) in 1982, according to a household survey commissioned by the National Institute on Drug Abuse.

This figure is down slightly from the 1979 survey, which reflects a lessening interest in marijuana and hallucinogenic (psychedelic) drugs. However, the use of stimulants by the under seventeen age group has increased 300 percent since 1979, according to Dr. Carlton Turner, Ph.D, special assistant to the president and director of the White House Drug Abuse Policy Office, referring to the survey.

This is alarming information about pervasive drug use and abuse by American teen-agers. But the results of the *Weekly Reader* classroom magazine survey of elementary school children are even more alarming according to the January 1983 issue. The survey reveals that 50 percent of our nation's fourth graders believed that their peers have experimented with drugs and 25 percent report "some" to "a lot" of peer pressure to try drugs or alcohol. In other words, the drug epidemic involves not just our teen-agers but even those under twelve years of age.

The use and abuse of illicit drugs and prescription drugs by children of any age is an issue of national concern!

Drug abuse shatters the dream of America as the most blessed and contented of nations. What is there about man that makes him so empty, so disillusioned in this age of affluence? Why has man never been satisfied with day-to-day existence? Why has he always been a difficult animal to please? His is a pervasive drive that is singularly human. Man is the only creature with the need to change his state of awareness, to alter private reality, to be beside himself.

I am a product of a fractured family—shattered by alcohol. For four years I was one of the thirty-six million Americans who experiment with illicit drugs and one of the thirteen to fifteen million who continued regular use.* Through my own exposure to thousands and thousands of teen-agers and because of my background, I see beyond the glitter of the contemporary "cool" drug scene.

As I travel, I am bombarded with questions and pleas from parents, ministers, teen-agers, and teachers who desire help. This book is a timely response to genuine needs. I am not a soap-box crusader, a noted psychologist, a behavioral scientist, or a notorious ex-drug pusher or junkie. This book is written by a young man who for four years was devoured by the "roaring lion," who found a solution and escaped, and whose greatest desire is to see that lion destroyed before it wrecks and ruins any more lives. I have

*1977 statistics

tried hard to prevent my personal prejudices from coming through and to present the evidence from all sides. It is my desire to be so thorough as to leave no stone unturned, yet not to produce a textbook filled with vague generalizations and of no practical value.

To make this revised edition even more helpful, review and application questions have been added to the end of each chapter. These have been aimed at the teen-ager who may be reading the book, but parents also can use them in discussions with their children.

I want to thank my dear friend Clayton Spriggs, who, I believe, is my Aaron and one of the most anointed men I've ever met for the hundreds of hours that he spends behind the scenes to make this ministry more fruitful. For his friendship, advice, and encouragement, I gratefully acknowledge the contribution he has made to my life and ministry. I would be remiss if I did not also thank JoAnn Spriggs for the hundreds of hours she spends in answering letters requesting help; these many hours she has spent are in service to our Lord. I am indebted to Freddie Gage, minister to the unreachables, for allowing me to use his materials and his experiences. Finally I thank R.O. and Angie Stone, who have shared their insights with me about their love and their real family.

In this land of affluence, millions are starving— starving for happiness and a life that isn't artificial or fake, starving for a life without drunkenness, pill-popping, shooting up, or pot smoking. This book is for those who desire to understand, to help, to rescue.

—Jay Strack

Drugs and Drinking

1.

Why Young People Turn to Drugs

THERE IS NO SINGLE CAUSE NOR SET of conditions that clearly leads to drug abuse. Those who use drugs often will not admit to doing so. However, the reasons usually given for drug-taking are: to feel in with the group; to feel good; to win the admiration of friends; to escape boredom; to have fun; to escape pressures; and to satisfy curiosity. Although we know much today about the dangerous and damnable effects of drugs and their abuses, the drug user himself still remains a mystery.

In general, drug abusers can be classified in three main groups. The first group consists of the *occasional users*. This includes the housewife who takes diet pills for extra energy to do household chores; the college student who uses amphetamines to stay up all night and study for exams; the truck driver or salesman who uses amphetamines to stay alert while driving all night; the executive who uses sleeping pills or tranquilizers to soothe the pressures of the day; the smoker who says he can—but can't—quit.

The second group is the *thrill seekers*. These are usually junior and senior high school and college-age people who use drugs just for the experience or so-called thrill of it. Because of this sporadic use, there is usually no physical addiction. Some thrill seekers may take drugs only once or twice and decide that drugs are a dead-end street or that there is more to life. The thrill seekers could be called "weekend users" because almost all their drug use is on weekends in groups or at parties. These recreational users include a large segment of the entire student population. In dealing with this group it is wise to remember that they consider themselves open-minded, critical, sensitive, aware, and hip.

For example, the great majority of cocaine users are social users who may take the drug for a specific purpose such as getting through exams or meeting a work deadline. What the social user may consider "harmless" is actually a dangerous trap. The drug gives a false sense of confidence and control that ultimately turns into a nightmare of uncontrol. No one sets out to become dependent on a drug, but it eventually happens to millions of social users.

The third group is the *addicts* or *junkies*. The addict's entire life rotates around the drug scene and drug experience. He exhibits strong psychological dependence (habituation) and physical dependence (addiction). Usually the junkie began to use drugs for the thrill, but now he is hopelessly dependent and does not believe he can function apart from the drug scene. His main objective in life is getting a continued supply, and this obsession frequently prevents him from continuing his education or job. He is often in trouble with his family, friends, and the law. The National Institute of Mental Health (NIMH) reports that drugs will cost the addict a loss of fifteen to twenty years of his life.

The great "turn-on" among millions of teen-agers can be attributed to several factors. Using the acronym PEACE, I will focus on the most frequent reasons for drug-taking given by teens across the country.

P ressure
E scape
A vailability
C uriosity
E mptiness

PRESSURE

Psychologists tell us that many youths turn to drugs for the sole purpose of belonging to the group. Clyde M. Narramore convincingly argues that teens desire peer-group approval more than parent or adult approval. They are preoccupied with being accepted by the gang, particularly since this is the age when family relationships may be strained.[1] It is evident that today's youth has substituted role conformation for goal attainment.

One of the teen-ager's greatest needs is to be accepted, not different or left out. The importance of popularity increases with the decline and fall of the family and home. It seems that every part of society is at war with the family. For example, the United States government and big corporations move fathers to new jobs across the country, uprooting entire families. This makes the "new kid on the block" easy prey for sexual advances and drug involvement because of the tremendous pressure to be accepted in the new place. With over one million divorces yearly and with twelve to fifteen million teen-agers living in broken homes, the drive to be accepted by teen-aged peers is increased.

My life is a good example of how peer pressure can lead to drug abuse. I come from a broken home, thanks to alcohol. Alcohol cost me my dad through divorce, my brother (because my mother could not provide financially for both of us), and my mother because she was forced to work two or three jobs. Needless to say, I hated alcohol and swore I would never drink it.

But in the seventh grade, on the way to my first dance, I was offered beer, along with the rest of the gang. Yes, I made my stand and said, "No way!" but after being called "chicken," "square," and "sissy," I gave in. Feeling as though I had lost my family, I was willing to try anything to be a part of the "in crowd." Any weak-willed teen-ager will follow the crowd, whether it leads to smoking, drinking, drugs, or immorality. The gang became my god; it determined my hairstyle, my mode of dress, my friends, and my attitudes toward school, church, and sex.

I have spoken to thousands of teens in schools, juvenile detention centers, jails, and churches; they all tell the same story—"I didn't want to be a chicken."

Recently in a Texas city, some teen-aged boys decided to play Russian roulette. The first boy tried once, fired, and luckily found the chamber empty. "Try it again," urged his pals. And so, after a few minutes he did. Again, a stroke of luck. "Man, you're really cool!" his friends told him. "Come on, do it again." This time the young man shakily refused to try his luck. The name-calling began: "You're chicken...yellow...you're just chicken." That young man gave in to his "friends," and this time his luck ran out. He died instantly.

Then there was the cute little girl who liked to play hide-and-seek. Some little boys told her to hide under a blanket in the bathtub. As she waited in the excitement, the boys happened to find a gun belonging to their dad. Playing and laughing, one boy challenged the other to shoot the little girl. The boy hastily refused and thought the idea horrible. The name-calling began—"You're chicken; you're scared," over and over. The pressure of name-calling caused that boy to give in angrily, and he emptied the revolver, putting all six bullets into the unsuspecting girl's body.

Rock concerts are good occasions to observe peer pressure and the tremendous need teens have to be accepted. Recently I went to a concert, and I found out things have changed much from when I filled my weekends with such concerts. These audiences are "families" where everyone is accepted. I noticed that the not-so-pretty girls, the chubby girls, boys with acne, and those who weren't athletes were all accepted; they belonged, and here they were cool. Their dress, their grades, and their hair didn't matter.

Of course, the pretty, the successful, and the popular teens also attend these concerts, but the point is that everyone belongs to this "family" that loves and accepts them the way they are. In this teen-aged herd, kids will do what everyone else is doing. Those who otherwise would never commit an immoral act or take a hard drug will probably do so here.

Dr. David Augsburger, in his relevant book *So What? Everybody's Doing It!*, gives several examples of the herd instinct. In 1978, a team of scientists were investigating the school instinct in fish. By a bit of skillful surgery, they removed a portion of a fish brain. After recovery, the fish was placed back in the tank with his original school. Soon the whole school began to follow this strange-acting fish with only part of a brain.[2]

When I am speaking at high schools I say, "The way of drug use is a crowd following someone with only half of a brain." Most of us have felt the tug of the herd instinct. In fact, it is so common that the English language needs about two dozen words just to name this drive that causes creatures to cluster and conform to one another. We talk of a flock of sheep, a pack of wolves, a swarm of bees, a covey of quail, a pride of lions, a gaggle of geese, a bevy of women, a gang of boys, or a herd of cattle. All these are expressions relating to the herd instinct which, when it appears among people, makes them dress, walk, talk, look, and even think alike.

Fourth graders across the United States report that they are perceiving peer pressure to start using drugs, according to a January 1983 survey published in the widely distributed *Weekly Reader* classroom magazine. Even more alarming is the fact that 50 percent of the fourth graders believe their peers have experimented with drugs, and that 25 percent report "some" to "a lot" of peer pressure to try drugs or alcohol.[3]

The National Institute on Drug Abuse conducted a 1983 survey of sixteen thousand seniors at 130 high schools. The results showed 5.5 percent as daily drug users; 63 percent had experimented with illegal drugs; 16 percent had some experience with cocaine; and 12 percent had tried heroin. The strong indication is that students are introduced to drugs by friends. The herd instinct is as unconscious and automatic as a reflex action.[4]

Every being has the need to associate with other living beings in order to form social attachments. This is illustrated in the story of the false killer whales that beached themselves on Florida's Loggerhead Key. Cetologists who studied the inner ear of a stranded false killer whale on that Key found a number of roundworms. According to the National Geographic Society, the scientists hypothesize that the worms may have damaged the whale's navigational organs. Even though he swam contrary to nature, the whole herd followed him to the beach.[5]

Studies indicate that the urge or drive for affiliation is especially intense when an individual is undergoing an anxiety-producing experience caused by problems at home or by physiological changes. This drive, also called the "gregariousness instinct," serves as a defense mechanism that operates on the principle of strength in numbers.

I challenge every teen: Be different! Wear a white hat. Dare to be great! Any dead fish can float with the current, but only a live, fighting fish can swim against the current. Anyone can be dirty and guilty and rebellious; it takes no real effort or determination I have noticed that great and honorable men don't travel in groups; they usually fly alone. Geese fly in gaggles and ducks fly in flocks, but an eagle soars high in the heavens—alone. How do you want to go through life? Honking and quacking? Or will you mount up with wings of strength and courage like eagles?

I am convinced that it takes more conviction to stand alone than to follow the crowd. All the trouble I got into as a teen-ager was with my crowd. We all decided to break into a home, or to harass a teacher, or to get drunk, and everyone joined in. Nature provides us with a tremendous example of the difference our herd makes.

A few years ago *National Geographic* magazine had a fascinating article called "Locusts: Teeth of the

Wind." The article depicted locusts as man's age-old adversary, the ravenous insects that in swarms caused the biblical famines. However, in 1921 Sir Boris Uvarov discovered that the terrifying locust begins life as a harmless green grasshopper.

In dry years, when bush vegetation is sparse, the grasshopper prefers to poke around independently without any companions. But, when heavy rains result in explosive breeding, the grasshopper's manner and appearance change. The insects constantly touch one another, and the resultant craving for company changes the grasshoppers' color to yellow, black, and red. Crowded together, they become aggravated and turn into varacious and destructive creatures.

In the Anti-Locust Research Center in London, an experiment revealed the change a touching herd causes in an individual grasshopper. A fan kept many tiny threads swirling inside a jar, simulating the touch of other grasshoppers. As the threads brushed the grasshopper, its color and behavior slowly changed.[6] Many a teen's attitude and behavior has been similarly altered by the crowd.

There is another type of pressure on youth to try drugs. We have already examined peer pressure, but now let us look at *pusher pressure*. Most adults don't realize that teen-agers can obtain virtually any type of booze, drug, or sexual thrill at their favorite youth hangout. Almost every drug imaginable is available in the restrooms of our public schools and in many private schools. These are startling statements, and I make them only after personally visiting many hangouts and schools across the country and learning the truth firsthand. I have been approached many times by sellers of illegal drugs.

The first time I ever used marijuana was when my friends and I went to the corner market to buy a bottle of booze, and the man said he wanted us to try something better. He had been our usual supplier for all kinds of liquor, selling it to underaged teens for a few dollars above retail. That is how it has started for millions of teens.

Most teens don't realize that illegal drugs are a multi-million-dollar business that often involves the underworld. However, it is important to destroy the myth that pushers are shabby, beady-eyed men in big overcoats who hang around the schools slipping drugs to our innocent little children. Most pushers are friends and contemporaries of teen-aged users. I began pushing by accident. I bought grass for myself, but soon discovered I could be popular with the crowd and make a few fast bucks by selling marijuana.

ESCAPE

America is looking for an escape from the ups and downs of everyday life. "To make things other than they are—through some kind of magic—that is the way of the drug addict. To wave a magic wand and repair the broken home, the nagging restlessness, the alienation, the neglect, omission, and deprivation. To wave a wand and efface the terrible sense of personal incompleteness."[7]

Millions of Americans are guilty of the "ostrich syndrome"—burying their heads in the sand, pretending that problems aren't really there. Millions escape through alcohol and drugs; this is a national catastrophe. Millions of barbiturates are swallowed every night to help us sleep. Millions of tranquilizers keep us calm during the day. And, yes, millions of pep pills and stimulants wake us in the morning. I call the drug trip "a flight from reality, a trip to nowhere."

Teens are turning on to escape the hassles of home, school, dating, and even the pressure that comes from physiological changes within them. The stresses on the adolescent who is coping with anger, sexuality, and an emerging identity can lead to drugs, which offer an alternative.

In order to understand why teens need to escape, it will be helpful to review some facts taught in basic psychology. Adolescence is the transitional stage in human development from the beginning of puberty to the attainment of the physical, emotional, and social maturity of adulthood. Most psychologists view it as the most stressful period of development in life. The adolescent must adjust to vast changes occurring rapidly within him after a long, peaceful period of relatively slow growth.

Many physiological changes cause confusion inside the teen. The pituitary gland, located at the base of the brain, controls growth and stimulates the hormonal activities of the sex glands. Both sexes begin to develop primary and secondary features of femininity and masculinity. Growth comes in spurts, and different parts of the body develop at different rates. These physical changes, including such problems as acne, have great psychological impact on the teen-ager. The self-image begins to change, and if the teen feels awkward or ugly (because of acne, overweight, underweight, under- or over-development), he tends to develop a poor self-image. Sexual feelings may also be overwhelming at this time. Since most parents fail to properly explain such feelings to their teens, it is understandable that the young people want to escape.

Many teens have never learned to accept themselves, and they feel lonely, unloved, depressed, and guilty. The drug scene offers an apparent escape that actually leads into a vicious cycle. Drug abuse only makes the problem worse. People get high to escape the guilt of past actions, but behavior while high may compound that guilt. Teens will commit acts while high that they would never have committed straight. So, in effect, the very problems teens want to escape— guilt, failure, family and school problems, frustration— are increased due to the drug dependence. This is the boomerang effect of drugs.

The rock group, The Eagles, in their hit song "Hotel California," sing, "Some dance to remember— some dance to forget." Not only is the drug experience an escape from reality, but often it is an escape from authority and responsibility. It also shows rebellion against many inconsistencies at home, school, and church.

Teens who are taking drugs begin to give in to the lure of the subculture or "the other world" experience. Many a teen has dropped out of the real world to go underground. This other world has its own language, values, speech, attitudes, goals, and even its own code of ethics. The effort to escape is so desperate that members of the subculture will give each drug ten or fifteen names just to confuse the straight world. Most teens are injured or destroyed not by life's dangers but by trying to escape reality.

AVAILABILITY

The easy access to every kind of drug at youth hangouts and in most school restrooms is another reason why so many are turning on. Teens are faced with the temptation almost every day and at almost every party. As we have already discussed, most kids know where to go and how to find the drugs they want. As I have shown, most kids are turned on to drugs by their own friends, and many first used drugs at school.

In one survey, 59 percent of high school seniors acknowledged having used marijuana. And quite clearly, they have little trouble getting it. A Gallup Poll found 81 percent of high school respondents saying marijuana was readily available.[8]

Not only do teens have easy access to all sorts of highs, but our affluent society helps them to be able to afford the drugs. An example of the availability of drugs is the magazine *High Times*. This is a slick publication aimed at promoting drugs and sex to the teen masses. It contains such articles as "All You Need to Know About Marijuana Botany," "Trans-High Market Analysis," (what type of drug to buy for the best high and the expected prices), "Trans-High Quotation Market," (a chart of prices on various drugs in the United States and nine other countries), and more. The High Times Bookstore offers *Cooking with Cannabis, How to Grow Marijuana Indoors*, and *How to Identify and Grow Psilocybin Mushrooms*, to name just a few. In addition, *High Times* prints a monthly schedule of smoke-ins, protests, pot conferences, etc. All this from the magazine which calls itself "The Magazine for 'High' Society."[9]

Although availability is not the only problem, it

certainly contributes heavily, as our teens are confronted by drugs everywhere they look.

CURIOSITY

Many teens want to try drugs for a new experience. According to the Arizona-based drug education program "Do It Now," 70 percent of teen-agers nationally and 90 percent of Arizona teens listed curiosity as the reason why they started taking drugs. I remember a young girl who came to our home to crash while on a bad trip. The next day I asked her why she had taken the drug (LSD) since I knew it was her first time. Her answer was, "I wanted to see a TV melt before my eyes."

Many teens get curious after listening to music that incorporates drug experiences and terms into songs created essentially for drug users. This is the reason most adults and non-drug users have a difficult time understanding much of today's rock music. Teen-agers hear this music all the time on the radio and even in movies. A bragging teen who is trying to act cool, psyched up, and describing the excitement of a high can cause his teen-aged friends to think, "Maybe I can have that, too."

Misguided curiosity seems to be one of Satan's favorite tricks. Curiosity, and a desire to experience the forbidden, ruined a blissful life for the first woman, Eve, and for mankind. Mythology teaches that Pandora's curiosity loosed evil upon the world. Even clichés remind us: "Curiosity killed the cat." The Bible warns, "Stolen waters are sweet, and bread eaten in secret is pleasant. But he knoweth not that the dead are there; and that her guests are in the depths of hell."[10] Forbidden fruit lures many to destruction.

EMPTINESS

The first four reasons give us some insight as to why teens try drugs, but this last is the reason millions stay on drugs. An emptiness seems to plague mankind. The Bible calls it being bankrupt in soul.[11] Although we are conquering our solar system, we have a void in our own inner space.

I believe the actions of youth and adults today reveal this emptiness. The epidemic of drugs, the flood of immorality, the rash of suicide attempts (about 2,000,000 last year, with the suicide rate tripling since 1955), the increase of divorce (50 percent of all children will live in a broken home at some time during their formative years), and the rising number of adherents to Eastern religions are all evidence of emptiness. The situation could be likened to a man trying to survive in a famine. When one is hungry and thirsty, he will do anything to stay alive. The story of the great famine that struck Samaria, as told in the Bible in 2 Kings 6:24–29, shows the desperation caused by famine. The head of a donkey was sold for "fourscore pieces of silver," and a mother even boiled and ate her own son.

A 1983 survey cited by the *Observer News* from the Johnson Institute found a high proportion of teen-agers who use alcohol or other drugs said they are trying to alleviate depression, loneliness, or anger. The burden is great on those who want to respond to this cry for help.

America is in a great spiritual famine. It is this aimless desperation and emptiness that has caused millions to hide behind a chemical curtain, drown in a sea of alcohol, or dive headfirst into the cesspool of fornication, adultery, and homosexuality. That emptiness drove me to try anything to fill that void in my life, including alcohol, drugs, cheap thrills, and even Eastern religion. An empty man is like a man writhing in pain, unable to find relief. An empty man doesn't know who he is, why he is here, or where he is headed. With no direction or goals, a teen resembles a ship adrift without a destination. He develops the "I-don't-care" attitude and a poor self-image. It is no great mystery that teens don't care or that they are so empty in this age of affluence. Even the institutions we hold dearest—the home, the church, and the school—are crumbling in their failure to meet natural and legitimate needs.

Simply stated, the destruction of authority seems to be the key to the problem. Liberal educators such as Dewey and Neill, with the help of the courts, took authority out of the schools by making discipline a thing of the past. Dr. Benjamin Spock, in his book *Baby and Child Care*, encouraged new parents to remove authority from the home. Liberal theologians have cut the heart out of the Bible, thereby removing authority from the church.

Human history began with a family. It was the first institution God created. When the earth was flooded in judgment, the new world began with the family of Noah. When God chose the nation of Israel as His own, He started it as a family. The family structure is so significant that the incarnation of Christ was set within the love of a family. The family structure is the foundation of our nation, and those who, for whatever reason, revolt against the family are revolting against the nation and against God.

It is little wonder that teens feel they are just existing instead of living. This emptiness also brings about spiritual and moral blindness. The Bible teaches that Satan, the god of this age, has blinded the spiritual eyes of those who don't know Jesus. Some teens turn on out of ignorance; they just don't know what they are getting into. (This seems incredible, considering all the effort towards drug education.) Most, however, are blinded by the glitter. Outside, the scene looks so good—the pounding music, the sensuous lyrics, the seductive dress of performers and participants; it promises escape from problems and rebellion without responsibility.

All the glitter covers up the fact that lives are ruined and destroyed. The undisciplined, empty life can lead to the neglect of studies and of physical well-being, to promiscuity and abortions, to accidents that cripple and bury friends. If you are going to follow the crowd, you had better find out where the crowd is headed. My emptiness led me to adopt the philosophy of "I'll try anything once." Mark it down: This attitude is a desperate cry for help.

Another evidence of emptiness is the restlessness of teens. I always had to be on the go, in a crowd with the music turned up full blast. Those in the field of human behavior tell us that restlessness is a sign of inner pain and insecurity. For a truly empty teen who has adopted an "anything-is-better-than-this" philosophy, drugs are a form of self-destruction.

In 1969 hundreds of thousands of teens gathered at a farm in New York state at an event known as Woodstock. Their chant was "drugs, sex, and rock and roll." This attitude still prevails in the lives of thousand of teens. Some of the rock stars of Woodstock are still popular today and have attempted to fill the emptiness of their lives with those three things. Some have been busted, some are burned out, and most are still searching for the answer to their emptiness. For several of the most popular, the search ended in tragedy. Janis Joplin sang, "Freedom's just another word for nothing left to lose," she died of a drug overdose. Jimi Hendrix, a phenomenon in his day, also died of a drug overdose. He sang, "There must be some way out of here" in one of his most popular songs. There was.

These attitudes still prevail. Money, popularity, adoring fans, success beyond measure have failed to satisfy these and many others. Comedian-actor John Belushi, well-known from "Saturday Night Live" on television, and movies such as "Animal House," died from speedballing (combining heroin and cocaine). Comedian Richard Pryor, thought by many to be among the brightest comedians of the day, almost burned to death while allegedly freebasing cocaine (smoking cocaine paste in a pipe). As the years pass, man dreams up new diversions, but his search to fill the emptiness of his soul continues.

I have been there, and I know there is nothing worse than emptiness. There is the constant search for self. I have often heard it said, "The longest journey is the journey inward." An empty teen is constantly searching for peace, pardon of past mistakes, purpose and power to live, and a life worth living.

The life of an empty teen is like a skydiver's jump: there are thrills for a while, but without a parachute he will hit hard. This was my situation for seventeen years.

By now I'm sure I've been labeled a pessimistic traitor for being so sour on my own generation. Let me say that I don't believe the majority of teens are rebels out to destroy the world, nor do I believe they are more evil than any other generation. Bob Seger, in his hit rock album "Night Moves," sums it up by singing about teens as being "young, restless, and bored." That is the most accurate appraisal of American teen-agers I have heard.

What Do You Think?

1. Define the three types of users and give a hypothetical example of each.
2. What do you feel is the strongest factor in a teen's decision to try drugs? Why?
3. Relate an account of when you or a friend gave into peer pressure. Also talk of a time when you resisted peer pressure. What do you think made the difference in your decisions?
4. Are drugs easily available to you? How? What do you think could be done to stop this easy access to drugs?
5. Do you personally feel an emptiness in your life? What steps have you taken or can you take to fill this emptiness? Is it a once-and-for-all answer to life or a continuing work on your part?
6. Take time to learn about the biblical examples of overcoming peer pressure as a young person. Study the lives of Joseph (Gen 37–50), Daniel (Dan. 1–6), Shadrach, Meshach, and Abednego (Dan. 2–3), and of course, Jesus Himself.

2.

Marijuana and Alcohol: America's Favorites

IS MARIJUANA MORE DANGEROUS THAN ALCOHOL?

THIS IS A POPULAR QUESTION TODAY. Freddie Gage, in his book *Everything You Wanted To Know About Dope*, states: "That is like asking if one would rather be bitten by a rattlesnake or a black widow spider. . . . Most of us would just as soon be bitten by neither."

Gage, who operated the highly successful Pulpit in the Shadows in Houston, Texas, gives these reasons why he feels marijuana is more dangerous than alchohol:

1. Hallucinations (the inability to distinguish between fact and fantasy) are more likely to occur with grass than with alcohol. For instance, under the influence of grass, a man might drive eighty miles per hour in a twenty-mile-per-hour zone because he actually feels like he is only going twenty miles per hour.
2. Muscular coordination is better with marijuana than with alcohol; therefore, dangerous impulses are more likely to result in action with marijuana than with alcohol.[1]

The effects of both grass and alcohol can be devastating. As you will see in the section on alcohol, it is one of the most dangerous drugs in the world. We know that alcohol is physically, psychologically, and socially dangerous for millions. The National Clearing House for Drug Abuse Information warns us that there is no firm evidence that marijuana would be any less harmful than alcohol if used consistently. In countries where alcohol is forbidden by religious taboo, skid rows still exist, largely the result of marijuana abuse. The drunk and the pot head are creatures to be pitied and helped.

Many feel that because alcohol is legal, marijuana should be also. With ten million alcoholics already living in a sea of booze, why add other mind-altering chemicals to our existing problem? There are already fifteen million people hiding behind a chemical curtain as it is. Increased availability of both drugs in America would be like a plague.

MARIJUANA

Abuse of marijuana is the most common drug problem in the United States today. Studies done over a decade ago often tried to minimize the dangers of the drug, but these studies are out of date. There has been a major change in the nature of marijuana being grown and sold today, and in the amount being used. The dangers of the drug have been grossly underrated. Marijuana used in the late 1960s and early 1970s had a comparatively low potency (less that one percent delta-9 THC). Thus the old data cannot be applied logically to today's marijuana, which is more potent and more frequently used.[2]

Marijuana is a drug found in the flowery tops and leaves of the Indian hemp plant (*cannabis sativa*). The flowering tops of the plant have the highest THC (tetrahydrocannabinol) resin. The leaves have a smaller amount, while the stalks and seeds have very little. Marijuana can be found just about anywhere, but the toxic component in the flowery tops is much stronger when the plant is grown in tropical climates.

The drug is called pot, tea, hemp, grass, and weed; the butt of a marijuana cigarette is called a roach. To be used as a drug, the leaves and flowers are cut, dried, and crushed into small pieces. This grassy-looking product is usually rolled into home-made cigarettes called joints. It can also be smoked in a pipe or baked in food. When I used marijuana, it became an ingredient in my favorite grass food, brownies.

The smoke from the joint is harsh, but sweet. Most adults don't recognize the smell, but as I travel throughout the country I smell it at schools, at youth hangouts, under the bleachers at ball games, and in public restrooms. It is not uncommon to see teen-agers passing joints among themselves while driving down the road. Often they will tell their parents it is a new incense they are burning.

Marijuana is usually sold by the joint or by the "lid." A lid is an ounce of refined marijuana and usually sells for thirty-five dollars up to one hundred dollars or more on today's market, depending on the type and strength. However, the lid may be cut with tobacco, tea leaves, oregano, or regular yard grass, and depending on supply and demand it may rise or fall in price considerably. An ounce of marijuana, depending on the desired strength and thickness of each joint, may be converted into twenty or thirty joints. The individual cigarettes are primarily sold at junior-high and high-school levels, where they cost from fifty cents to a dollar each.

Although marijuana has been smoked for more than five thousand years, it has never been more popular than today. In 1920, the use of marijuana as an intoxicating drug was introduced into the United States. In 1937, its general use was outlawed by the Federal Marijuana Tax Act, which was followed by strict laws and enforcement. In the 1960s, pot's popularity bloomed. Its use was initially confined to a small minority characterized by counterculture orientation, for whom it was a symbol of opposition to the "establishment." But today's users come from a broad cross section of American youth.

When grass is smoked, the effect usually begins in about fifteen minutes and lasts from two to five hours. The potency of the drug is dependent on the climate in which it is grown, the soil, the time of harvesting, and other conditions. Some marijuana may have no effect whatsoever. The THC content of the plant determines its mind-altering ability. Most of the marijuana grown in the United States is low in THC content. Many teens make do with a poor-quality grade grown in the States and in Mexico. The grade is far below that of the famous "Acapulco Gold" or "Panamanian Red." The states bordering Mexico and the Gulf of Mexico usually have more potent grass.

Good marketing procedures dictate that the best grass (most potent) goes to the big city markets and then to university cities. What most teens are ignorant of is that each time grass passes hands, it is cut and adulterated with such things as yard grass, catnip, and fertilizer. As with poor LSD, pushers will doctor the poor pot with chemicals rather than lose money. It must be cured in, soaked in, or sprayed with a hallucinogen to enable the user to get high on what the pushers call "trash." This is what many of the smaller towns in the South and Midwest end up getting.

Because of this practice, teen-agers who would ordinarily never experiment with chemicals are putting damaging chemicals into their bodies without realizing it. The user begins to feel high, as he would after a few alcoholic drinks. This can cause him to experience one of two conditions. He may become very happy, talkative, loud, and experience uncontrollable hilarity and fantasy. This makes him feel that he is above reality and that he has a greater appreciation of art and music. The user's sense of time and distance may become distorted. A minute may seem like hours or the next room may seem miles away. On the other hand, the user may feel just the opposite. He may become irritable and confused or fearful. Instead of being "super high," he can become drowsy and unsteady, finding it difficult to coordinate his movements. It should be said that, regardless of the effects on an individual, grass always affects his judgment.

A user of marijuana finds it harder to make decisions, and he is easily swayed by the crowd. Even though marijuana has no aphrodisiac properties, promiscuity seems to increase among those using it. Our crowd of teens would always offer our dates a few drinks or some grass because these would weaken the girls' judgment and lower their resistance. Probably it is the combination of boredom, music, wine, marijuana, and the crowd that actually causes immorality to increase rather than just the grass alone.

The National Institute on Drug Abuse has sponsored more than one thousand experimental projects concerning marijuana. Prominent among the findings in these documents are that marijuana use impairs memory, learning and speech, reduces ability to perform tasks such as driving or flying, has negative effects in terms of heart rate and lung capacity, introduces cancer-causing hydrocarbons into the lungs, may affect the reproductive functions, leads to psychological problems in youthful users, induces feelings of paranoia and can lead to panic anxiety reactions. Regular use—even once or twice a week—means the user is never entirely free of the drug.[3]

Marijuana is not an addictive drug; that is, it does not lead to physical dependence or to subsequent withdrawal symptoms. However, users can become psychologically dependent. Most regular users don't want to function without a "little help from their friends," which are drugs. I would smoke a joint before school, during a break, during lunch, and right after school. There was a period of more than three years when I would never go out to a party, a game, or a date without being high. Marijuana easily becomes a psychological and emotional crutch, and it is difficult to quit the "mind" habit.

While the marijuana user may become violent, generally he is passive. Sometimes the law is broken by a person under marijuana influence, but it is usually a traffic violation. The personality of the user is as important as the type of drug used in determining whether drug use will lead to criminal or violent behavior.

Studies do show that high-school users, as compared to non-users, place less value on achievement and higher value on independence. They tend to be more alienated and critical, more tolerant of deviance, less religious, less influenced by parents than by friends, and poorer students.

People are always asking, "Does marijuana lead to other drugs?" Nothing in marijuana itself leads to other drugs. However, in my own experience—and most surveys and research books confirm this—grass users tend to try other drugs; thus grass becomes a steppingstone. A young boy may try marijuana and like it; after a while, in the same environment that led to that first drink or that first joint, he'll get curious about other highs. He may try barbiturates, speed, and on and on.

Some of the country's most prestigious institutions of higher learning, after years of study, are concluding that the use of marijuana does lead to other drugs. Marijuana seems to serve as a drug that initiates the user into his or her first experience with behavior altering substances. Once a person has tried marijuana it then becomes easy to go on to something else that is more exciting, gives greater stimulation, or is more illicit.

Every junkie I have ever met started with marijuana. You see, the danger is in enjoying the "high," the dropping out. Soon the mild high grows boring, and the user goes on to something more exciting. There is no direct cause-and-effect link between grass and harder drugs, but the drug user is exposed to other drugs and encouraged by the pusher and other users. The marijuana smoker's psychological make-up may cause him to seek other drugs; when grass does not meet his needs, he looks aound for a pill that does.

One source I have used feels that once a person breaks the law by becoming involved in illegal activities, he is already on his way downhill. The Phoenix House in New York, a drug addict rehabilitation center, reports that 398 out of 400 addicts started with marijuana. Nine out of ten heroin users, sometimes more depending on the study quoted, but never less, used cannabis (marijuana) first. They found it was not sufficient to solve their ego-inadequacies and stepped up to something more suited for emotional needs.

The use of marijuana is definitely on the increase. A national survey on the lifestyles and values of high school seniors as related to drugs informs us that the use of marijuana continues upward. This study is significant because it represents an attempt to examine the change in attitudes and behavior during the critical years of late adolescence and young adulthood. Since this survey taps both drug-using behavior and attitudes toward drugs, it provides us with a barometer of regrettable future trends.

ALCOHOL

Alcohol is the most widely used psychoactive drug in North America. The National Council on Alcoholism estimates there are nearly ten million alcoholics in the United States. According to the *Journal of the American Medical Association*, this is robbing our nation of ten million brains. Almost 70 percent of

Americans drink some mixture of alcohol. *The Journal* also reports that only 3 percent of the total number of people suffering from alcoholism in the United States are found on skid row. Ninety-seven percent are generally found in factories, offices, or schools.

Alcoholism is America's third largest health problem, following heart disease and cancer. It afflicts ten million people, costs sixty billion dollars, and is implicated in two hundred thousand deaths annually. Alcohol is involved in 50 percent of deaths by motor vehicle and fire, 67 percent of murders, and 33 percent of suicides. It contributes to morbidity in certain malignancies and to many diseases of the endocrine, cardiovascular, gastrointestinal, and nervous systems.[4]

It is difficult to think of alcohol as a drug in our culture, but it is a dangerous one for millions of people. This particular drug is the most ancient, most widely enjoyed, and the most extensively misused of all drugs known to man. Man first became acquainted with alcohol when fruit juice was left open to the air and fermented. This fermentation was the work of a group of microscopic, one-celled fungi—the yeasts—which are present on the skins of fruit and float by the millions in the air we breathe.

Ethyl alcohol can be produced synthetically or naturally by fermenting fruit, grain, or vegetables. Here in the United States, millions consume alcohol in the form of beer, wine, and hard liquor. In fact, the cocktail party may be the most common form of organized drug-taking in the Western world.

When alcohol is absorbed into the bloodstream it acts as a depressant on the central nervous system. As with any central nervous system depressant, it slows reflexes and thinking processes and affects coordination. It is distributed uniformly, microscopically, and enters the brain easily. The rate of absorption depends on both the kind of drink and on the contents of the stomach.

Alcohol disrupts communication in the brain. The most complex circuits are affected first, including those involved in logical thinking, problem solving, and judgment. And, as judgments in general become less balanced and well considered, so, too, do judgments about one's own behavior. Behavior becomes more impulsive and the drinker's control of his or her behavior decreases as the alcohol intake increases. The environment will also affect the drinker's actions.[5]

The range of physical reactions to varying doses of alcohol is vast. One or two drinks may induce talkativeness or slight flushing and might also reduce a drinker's inhibitions so that he appears more open, responsive, and emotional. But in another individual, this same amount may induce drowsiness, depression, and lethargy. Later doses can alter perception, cause staggering, blurred vision, and other manifestations of drunkenness. While one person may become emotional or amorous, another may become aggressive and hostile.

In pregnant women alcohol crosses the placental barrier into the fetus. Contrary to the old wives' tale that wine and beer make strong babies, the fact is that alcohol is a threat to unborn babies. The National Institute on Alcohol Abuse and Alcoholism has released strong warnings based on studies that show that pregnant women who take more than two drinks a day run the risk of bearing mentally retarded or physically deformed babies.

Withdrawal from alcohol typically involves loss of appetite, sleeplessness, vomiting, hallucinations, and tremors. Impending DTs (*delirium tremens*) mark the beginning of the withdrawal syndrome. It should be noted that steam baths, coffee, cold showers, or exercise are not significant "sobering up" agents because they have little effect on the rate of the alcohol's metabolism.

Not only does alcohol have a tremendous physical effect that may cause physical dependence, but psychological dependence is also generally a major part of the alcohol problem. In the fascinating book *Alcoholics Anonymous*, called "The Big Book" by members of that organization, at least one hundred illustrations and testimonies of alcoholics tell how they started the day with a drink to escape their worries and problems. Sometimes they became drunk deliberately, feeling justified by nervousness, anger, worry, depression, or jealousy. Psychological dependence is often the most difficult area to treat in alcoholism.

It is helpful to remember that an alcoholic must be freed from his physical craving for liquor before psychological measures can take effect. This often requires a hospital procedure of detoxification ("drying out").

The Personal Cost of Alcohol

1. In addition to adult problem drinkers, it is estimated by the National Institute on Alcohol Abuse and Alcoholism that 19 percent of adolescents (fourteen to seventeen years of age) or 3.3 million youths are problem drinkers.[6]

2. Alcohol has been a major disrupter of family life. It has been found that 60 percent of marriages

in which one or both partners are alcohol-dependent will end in divorce or separation. Children of parents who drink excessively often are afflicted by neglect, persecution, and physical attacks upon them. As a result of their disorganized childhood, 55 percent become alcoholics themselves.[7]

3. The failure to control one's behavior and the depression evident during drinking are reasons why the suicide rate of alcoholics has been found to be six to twenty times higher than that of the general population in various studies.[8]

4. Chronic alcoholism causes brain damage, nerve damage, and pancreas damage. Cirrhosis of the liver is now the fourth leading cause of death among males age fifty-five to sixty-five, and among males twenty to forty it is the third fastest growing cause of death, ranking next to heart disease and lung cancer. Resistance to infection is also impaired, and pneumonia and tuberculosis are not uncommon among heavy drinkers. Alcohol addicts have been found to sustain higher than average rates of cancer of the liver, throat, and upper gastrointestinal tract. The average lifespan of a heavy drinker is shortened by eleven years.

5. Many drinkers also suffer from vitamin deficiency, sexual impotence, and infections. Not only are these costly to the body, they affect the emotional balance. Chronic drinkers suffer from a loss of memory and mental confusion. One-fifth to one-quarter of all admissions to psychiatric hospitals are for chronic alcoholism.

6. Alcohol is labeled a drug because it has the capacity to alter the mind and become both habit forming and physically addictive. Heavy drinking causes intolerance, craving, and a withdrawal state involving DTs, which are very violent and painful.[9]

Social Costs

1. Alcohol provokes violent behavior more frequently than any other drug. In 90 percent of all assaults and 50 to 60 percent of all rapes and homicides, the aggressors were found to be under the influence of alcohol. In fact, police statistics across the nation reveal that one-third to one-half of all arrests are alcohol related.[10]

2. Studies show that 10 percent of drivers involved in accidents resulting in minor property damage and 15 percent of drivers involved in extensive property damage have a raised blood alcohol concentration of 0.5 percent. One-fourth of drivers in crashes resulting in serious injury and one-half of the drivers in fatal crashes are legally drunk. Of single vehicle crashes occurring on weekend nights, 10 percent of the drivers are intoxicated. If these figures are applied to National Safety Council data, that means twenty-six thousand deaths and five hundred thousand disabling injuries due to vehicle accidents each year involve drunken drivers.[11]

3. "Alcohol and sex have a long, deep, and enduring relationship through many ages and many cultures," writes Ann Geller, M.D., director of the Smithers Treatment Center of St. Luke's-Roosevelt Hospital in New York City. Experiments show that

as alcohol intake increases so does interest in sexual activity. In general, small amounts of alcohol create a euphoric feeling that might increase sexual arousal. That feeling may help the drinker to relax and overcome inhibitions that would otherwise cause the drinker to reject or control sexual advances or activity. My feeling is that alcohol is a major factor in the epidemic of teen pregnancies for unmarried girls.[12]

4. Alcohol is the major factor in the emotionally damaging father-daughter incest occurrences.[13]

As of 1974, more than 250,000 persons die each year from alcohol, its illnesses, and related crimes. With this damaging evidence, if alcohol were to be presented for legalization as a drug today, it surely would not be accepted.

Teen-age Drinking

Almost every school survey indicates that alcohol and tobacco are the first and most frequently used drugs among adolescents.

Several factors make it difficult for teens to decide whether or not to drink alcoholic beverages.

Pressure of the adult role model—The adult culture is putting tremendous pressure on teens in very subtle ways. We have already seen that more than 70 percent of Americans drink some type of alcohol. It seems that drinking denotes adult status. Psychologists tell us there is tremendous pressure to be a "real man" or a "real woman." Many teens feel alcohol provides a shortcut to maturity. Every time we take a drink, we are giving our children permission to drink.

A five-year study of drinking on television reveals that alcohol is the preferred beverage used by characters. Viewers are exposed to more than eight alcohol drinking events per hour, and that the rate of this activity is rising. All kinds of characters were observed drinking, with the exception of youth. Once again, the adult role model is presented to our children.[14]

Pressure of advertising media—Drinking is glamorized and promoted by attractive advertising. The multi-billion-dollar-a-year profit of the alcoholic beverage industry enables it to pour millions into mind-manipulation. In fact, according to the U.S. Commerce Department, in 1981 newspapers received ninety-five million dollars in advertising from the beer and wine industry; television received three hundred and three million dollars in advertising money in 1982; and magazines sold ads for alcohol to the tune of two hundred fifty-eight million dollars.[15] Thanks to the mass media, drinking is portrayed as socially acceptable.

Virtually all alcohol advertising employs subliminal (unconscious or subconscious) stimuli. Such phrases as "You only go around once in life, so grab all the gusto you can" present alcohol as an alternative to the everyday routine of life. One of the booze industry's more cynical attacks upon the young appeared recently in a public relations poster distributed throughout the world. It portrayed two eighteen-year-olds, both clean-cut, neat, and mature-looking. The caption read: "You're old enough to drink. Are you mature enough?" How many teen-agers will reply, "Of course I'm mature enough. My parents think I'm an irresponsible child, but I'll show them my maturity by drinking"? Most of the early-life conditioning to accept alcohol is media induced. One facet of American culture, cleverly exploited by the alcoholic beverage industry, involves the identification of masculinity with drinking. Virtually all young men in America are taught that "holding your liquor" is a sign of manhood.

Beer and liquor are advertised as part of the "good life." The cool, swinging, mature, sensuous, and athletic crowds all drink. What satanic deceit! Follow those people home from a party, and watch the glitter turn into emptiness.

Pressure of associates—In Chapter 1, we discussed the tremendous impact peer decisions have on teens. A dangerous chain reaction of experimentation with alcohol is working its way through our schools.

What Others Say About Alcohol

"First the man takes a drink,
then the drink takes a drink,
then the drink takes a man..."
　　　—Iapanese proverb

"The drunken man is a living corpse."
　　　—St. John Chrysostom

"Alcoholism is drinking to escape problems created by drinking..."
　—panelist at Yale Center of Alcohol Studies

"Alcoholism is reached when certain individuals stop bragging about how much they can drink and begin to lie about the amount they are drinking..."
　　　—American Medical Association

"One drink is too many. Twenty is not enough."
—skid-row alcoholic in medical interview

"O God, that men should put an enemy in their mouth to steal away their brains."
                              —William Shakespeare

"Drunkenness is the ruin of reason. It is premature old age. It is temporary death."
                              —St. Basil

"Alcohol is a cancer in human society, eating out the vitals and threatening destruction."
                              —Abraham Lincoln

"Drunkenness has killed more men than all the history's wars."
                              —General Pershing

"To put alcohol in the body is like putting sand on bearings of an engine. It doesn't belong."
                              —Thomas Edison

The Bible Says...

"At the last it [alcohol] biteth like a serpent, and stingeth like an adder" (Prov. 23:32).

"Let us walk honestly, as in the day; not in rioting and drunkenness..." (Rom 13:13).

"Envyings, murders, drunkenness...they which do such things shall not inherit the kingdom of God" (Gal. 5:21).

Researchers have found that people usually don't leap into drug use. They start slowly. The lure is subtle. In fact, some experts feel that if early use of cigarettes and alcohol can be discouraged then there will be no problem later with the use of other drugs. It is better to form good habits than to reform bad ones.

Despite heated debates about whether marijuana or any other drug is a steppingstone to heroin, every survey I have reviewed found alcohol to be the first mind-altering drug used by teen-agers.

With all the evidence about alcohol pointing to potential destruction for its users, the question still arises, "Why not drink socially?" My answer is this: Drinking alcohol is one of the most unsociable acts committed; it disorients its user from himself, his family, and those around him. Instead of urging our young not to *begin* the use of mind-altering drugs, we merely warn "not too much" when they don't even know what too much is. We are doing too little too late.

What Do You Think?

1. Which is the greatest problem in your area—marijuana or alcohol?
2. Should marijuana be legalized? If it should someday be legalized, would this give the Christian permission to use it? Why or why not?
3. Based on the experiences of those around you and the information in this book, do you feel marijuana is a steppingstone to other drugs?
4. What are some of the dangers of marijuana? Is the physical danger its greatest harm to the user?

Name at least three changes you feel marijuana brings about in a person.

5. Do you feel that alcohol should be labeled as a drug? Give at least three reasons to support your conclusion.
6. What is the greatest influence on a teen to drink alcohol, other than peer pressure? Do TV ads and magazine advertisements for beer and wine affect the thinking of teen-agers?
7. Review pages 40–50 and memorize at least two scriptures concerning alcohol use.

3.

Cocaine: The Feel-Good Drug

COCAINE, THE CENTRAL NERVOUS system stimulant once called the "rich man's drug," is now the drug of daily choice for four to five million Americans, without regard to economic status. During the past two years the number of Americans using cocaine has dramatically increased—from 15 million to 22 million—and is still rising. In fact every day some five thousand people try cocaine for the first time, seduced by the drug's reputation, however false it is.[1] These people cannot be written off as crazy adolescents. Government studies find that those in their late twenties and in their thirties constitute the fastest growing proportion of users.

The prevailing mood of "live for self and pleasure" encourages impressionable young people to experiment with cocaine. Christopher Lasch wrote in his book, *The Culture of Narcissism,* "To live for the moment is the prevailing passion—to live for yourself, not for your predecessors or posterity. We are fast losing the sense of belonging to a succession of generations originating in the past and stretching into the future. It is the waning of the sense of historical time—in particular the erosion of any strong concern for posterity." This perceptive observation describes the spiritual crisis of the seventies and holds true for the eighties. This is especially true of the students and teens, among whom cocaine is spreading rapidly. This is a tragedy. Youth have the greatest need to believe in the future and to trust in posterity.

It is time to wipe away the glitter of cocaine. Thomas B. Kirkpatrick of the Illinois Dangerous Drug Commission says, "My guess is that we are only half way there. The use of coke will probably double before we see any decline in its popularity."

Once, I visited a home to share the gospel. When a small girl came to the door and invited me in, I walked into a room where her parents were arguing with each other while the father, a successful executive, scratched the floor like a dog, trying to pick up any last flakes of cocaine that had been spilled. The drug was his master.

A young girl called me from jail to tell me she had been arrested for wandering nude on the beach. It was later discovered she had been high on cocaine. In shame and tearful remorse she told me she didn't remember a thing about how she got there or who she was with.

Today's young, talented comedians can make jokes and offer innuendos about cocaine, but the truth is anything but funny.

Cocaine is a powerful psychoactive drug that works as a central nervous system stimulant and produces excitement, restlessness or artificial energy, and gives a false sense of intense euphoria. This stimulant causes its desired effects by a number of interactions with the brain. Its initial effect on the body is to raise the blood pressure by constricting the circulatory system and increasing the rate of respiration. By narrowing the blood vessels, cocaine acts upon the heart and circulatory system, increasing the heart rate, which then causes irregular heart beats, shortness of breath and angina.

There are three basic methods of ingesting cocaine. The most popular is snorting. This is done by rolling paper or a dollar bill into a tube and then inhaling the powder into one nostril through the tube. The drug also is cooked into a liquid and intravenously injected.

The third, and possibly the most dangerous, method also gives the most intense high. It is called freebasing. As cocaine is just one distilled component of the coca leaf, cocaine freebase comes from carrying the refining process one ill-advised step further. The active drug is "freed" from its "base," a hydrochloride salt. Extraction techniques involve dissolving the cocaine and adding chemical catalysts—sodium hydroxide and ether or, more prudently, baking soda—that cause the freebase to separate. The remaining solid, about half a gram from each gram of regular coke, is filtered or skimmed off and dried. It is then smoked in a small glass water pipe, often filled with rum instead of water. The user inhales the vapor and, in seconds, gets a sensation that lasts about a minute and is gone within ten.[2]

Why Is It So Popular?

The question asked by so many is "why?" What can make so many types of people flock to a dangerous drug? Aside from the problems I discussed in "Why Young People Turn to Drugs," cocaine offers its own seduction. On the surface, it appears to be a supremely beguiling and relatively risk-free drug. At least this is what its devotees claim. A snort in each nostril offers thirty minutes of euphoria. The user perceives himself as alert, witty, exciting, and in control. He has no hangover to deal with, believes no addiction will result, has no concern of lung cancer or burned out cells in the brain, and is not left with telltale needle marks in the arms or legs. The user may feel he has found the "perfect" drug, when, in fact, the dark and destructive side of cocaine is just beginning to make itself known.

The mood of the sixties and seventies was to "turn on and drop out." Today's mood is one of sophistication and achievement. Cocaine offers these to the blue-collar as well as the white-collar worker. The demand to perform seems to be helped along by the rush of the cocaine snort, without thought to the depression that may follow. It's a feel-good drug with a dangerous ending.

Dr. Mark Gold, director of research at Fair Oaks Hospital, Summit, New Jersey, and originator of the national hot line for help with cocaine questions (800-COCAINE), said that since the service was begun in May 1984 calls have been coming in at a rate of from six hundred twenty-five to twelve hundred a day. Of three hundred random interviews, the average age of the callers was twenty-nine, but their ages spanned from fourteen to the late sixties.

Cocaine is used for the same basic reasons and effects that other drugs are used for—to escape from our own imperfections and insecurities and from the discomfort or pain of reality. However, cocaine users fail to see themselves as they are. Since most are generally success-oriented and desire to outshine the rest, they do not use cocaine to cope or get by, but rather to go beyond the expectations of family, friends or society, even if only in their imaginations. The euphoric effects of cocaine are well known. Cocaine users tend to be the go-getters. The users tend to have the perfect illusion for twenty or thirty minutes—they are smarter, sexier, more competent, more masterful than anyone else. It has been called the "ego-food."

What Are the Dangers?

Cocaine is supposed to make you feel great; and, in truth, temporarily it does. But soon it enslaves and numbs the user. The book *Snow Blind* has an almost perfectly accurate title. Few cocaine users see themselves in reality; few can see the physical, psychological, emotional, and often familial damage crippling their lives. One young user confessed, "After one hit of coke, I feel like a new man. The only problem I have is that the first thing the new man wants is another hit of coke."

Clearly, coke is no joke. The euphoric lift, the self-confidence and control felt after a snort is followed by an intense letdown. Regular use can induce depression, edginess and weight loss. As usage increases, so does the danger of paranoia, hallucinations, physical collapse and total devastation of the nasal membrane. The user feels blessed with a sense of indestructibility. Later, he feels totally destroyed.

Gold's random survey of 800-COCAINE callers noted that over 75 percent of them reported chronic symptoms—loss of energy, insomnia, loss of sex drive (even though sex is often given as a reason for use), and trembling and heart palpitations. All complained of jitteriness, anxiety, irritability and depression; over 75 percent complained of paranoia and loss of interest in non-drug activities. In addition, three-quarters of the users said they must take alcohol to "calm down."

Without question, one of cocaine's biggest risks is that it detours people from normal pursuits; it often entraps and redirects the user's activities into almost total preoccupation with the drug. This, of course, becomes extremely expensive and new financing must be arranged.

Gold discovered the several options for obtaining drug money. More than 25 percent reported that they had stolen from family, friends or their workplace to support their habit. He said that most start out by stealing from their families because it is relatively easy, but then move on to stealing from their employers. There are also many users who seek out jobs where it is easy for them to steal, or who turn down promotions so they can remain in a position where stealing is not difficult. Approximately 40 percent felt they had to sell drugs to support their habit. About half reported job problems.

Is Cocaine Addictive?

Unfortunately, the addiction of cocaine is real, but it is so coy and deceptive that few ever realize the addiction until they are trapped. Until recently, scientific knowledge about cocaine use was very limited and most of it was based on studies more than fifty years old. Because of this, coke has enjoyed a far better reputation than it deserves. There is now new evidence that the drug is addictive, harmful, and sometimes fatal.

Heroin or alcohol addiction is fairly easy to determine—physical pain and suffering accompany any withdrawal. While cocaine does not produce the physical symptoms of narcotic withdrawal, continued use by snorting, injection or freebasing can lead to severe dependency. Those who tout the safety of cocaine say it is not addictive in the classic sense associated with alcohol and marijuana. For this reason the term "addiction" must be clearly defined.

An addictive drug is one that can produce in a significant number of people at least three conditions: 1) compulsion, 2) loss of control, 3) continued use of the drug in spite of adverse effects. Compulsion is evident when the person who is offered cocaine or who has access to cocaine cannot refuse the urge to use it. Loss of control is likened to the alcoholic who goes on a weekend drunk. The drug totally determines his schedule, leading to exhaustion and physical collapse. Continued use in spite of consequences is the ultimate loss of control: stealing or dealing drugs to support the habit; using cocaine regardless of its effect on your health; chronic use even after being exposed or having made the decision to stop. The addicted cocaine user knows he is getting in deeper and deeper by allowing cocaine to be the obsession of his life.[3]

Dr. Gabriel G. Nahas of Columbia University College of Physicians and Surgeons, New York, has written a brochure entitled *Cocaine, The Great Addicter.* In it he offers the following information which points out the dangers of addiction to cocaine, even though it may bend the standard definition of "addiction":

1. Fatal overdoses of cocaine either snorted or injected have been regularly reported and are on the increase. Death is caused by heart failure or respiratory paralysis; convulsions also occur.
2. Chronic effect: The frequent snorting of cocaine produces burns and sores of the membranes that line the interior of the nose. Ear and nose specialists see more and more frequently, in habitual cocaine users, perforations of the septum, the cartilage separating the nostrils.

3. Physical symptoms of heavy cocaine use include cold sweats, pallor, uncontrolled tremors, a sensation of heaviness of the limbs, aggressive behavior, insomnia and weight loss.

4. Psychological symptoms are characterized by intense anxiety, depression and confusion, hallucination (the conviction that ants are crawling under one's skin, for example) and paranoia. These latter symptoms often require hospitalization in a psychiatric ward.

5. Rapid, marked tolerance develops to cocaine use (making it necessary to increase the dosage in order to obtain the initial effect).

6. Cocaine and amphetamines are the only drugs that laboratory animals will administer to themselves repeatedly until they die. This is solid proof of the behavioral dependence created by cocaine, which has been called the great addicter because of the profound craving that it creates in the brain of the user.[4]

Dr. David Smith, Director of Haight-Ashbury Free Medical Clinic in San Francisco has said, "Cocaine is very addicting." Dr. Mitchell Rosenthal of the highly successful Phoenix House Drug Treatment Center has stated, "Of all the drugs, cocaine is the most difficult to deal with."

The message of modern cocaine research, then, is clear: cocaine is dangerous. And, while some people can experiment with it, for others the prognosis is bleak. One recovering cocaine addict described it this way: "We're all on a plane flying around over Kansas. We're going to give everyone a knapsack. Some contain parachutes and some do not. Now, who would like to jump out of the plane? It's really fun if your parachute opens."[5]

Where Does Cocaine Come From?

The cocaine trail to the United States begins over twenty-five hundred miles southwest of Florida, on the eastern slopes of the Andes Mountains. The "scrubby little plant" itself has become the center of a multi-billion-dollar illegal industry. The cash crop is grown primarily between Bolivia and Peru, but the business is controlled by Colombians who transform the gooey coca paste for final refining into crystalline white cocaine. This is accomplished by soaking raw coca leaves in various chemicals and oil. The resulting muddy brown paste is purified into so-called coca base, a dirty-white, almost colorless substance that is shipped to Colombia for the refining process.

From the jungles of South America to the noses of desirous Americans, the trade is almost entirely controlled by Colombians. For several thousand years the South American Indians cultivated and chewed the leaves of the coca plant. It was used as medicine to relieve stomach pains, to anesthetize toothaches, and to help laborers endure long hours of strenuous work under a blazing sun. In 1859 the coca plant was imported to Europe and in 1860 the drug cocaine was isolated from the plant.

For the next fifty years cocaine was legal and popular in the United States and Europe. It was sold in wine and was the active ingredient in the soft drink Coca Cola until 1906. Sigmund Freud briefly experimented with the drug and treated patients' depression with it. It is reported that Robert Louis Stevenson wrote *The Strange Case of Dr. Jekyll and Mr. Hyde* in six days while under the influence of cocaine. The use and popularity of cocaine diminished until the late sixties when the drug culture brought back its popularity.

Today it is a twenty-five billion-dollar business in this country, run primarily by the underworld. Of all the drugs in the United States, cocaine is now the biggest producer of illegal income. If all the international wholesale dealers who supply the drug to the United States market were to form a single corporation, it would probably rank seventh on the *Fortune* 500 list, between Ford Motor Company and Gulf Oil Corporation.

This drug usually is smuggled into the United States by the ton in private planes and boats. Smaller amounts are brought in by individuals, who hide it in clothing, instruments, half-eaten candy bars, artifacts, feed sacks, and even in plastic sacks in their stomachs, which occasionally burst, causing death.

How to Get off Coke

Cocaine is big business because at first it makes you feel great, energetic, smart, sexy and in charge of life. But with hundreds of deaths each year and thousands of families, careers and futures being destroyed (maybe yours), you know it is no longer safe to use. Can a person die from cocaine use? The answer is yes, and in many ways. Personal tolerances and the method of use are key factors in determining a fatal dose. The fatal dose of cocaine is said to be about one thousand milligrams, although smaller doses have caused death. Death is fairly rapid in most cases, usually through convulsions and heart and lung failure; it can occur to snorters, injectors and freebasers. Death can also come as a result of heart attack, stroke or arrhythmia. Suffocation and drowning in one's own secretions can occur as well. A new study has made researchers suspicious that lung damage is possible from cocaine freebasing.

Gold states that most of the hot-line callers feel

after a self-examination and evaluation that they are in serious trouble or even addicted. Cocaine is a sly drug. It has a habit of sneaking up on you. The drug's ability to make you feel aware, confident and secure may blind you to the fact that you are gradually losing control over your drug-taking. No one sets out to be a statistic, but it happens.

Get Smart—You have already taken this step by realizing you have a problem: you are dependent on the drug and have decided to do something about it. This is the first step to getting off any drug, and it is especially true of cocaine. This is the step I had to take when I wanted to escape my meth-crystal habit. It was not easy for me to do because drugs were my whole life and because they brought intense pleasure. It likewise will be hard for you to imagine life without coke. In fact, unless you move away from your friends, the drug will be everywhere—work, school, spa or night spots. Remember, you cannot handle coke. This is not a sign of weakness, but rather the recognition of this fact is a show of strength. You are now taking charge of your life again. Throw away the crutch. You can shine on your own; you don't need the "boost" anymore. They don't call cocaine the "ego drug" for nothing.

Get Help—Go see a doctor. Do not be embarrassed about talking to your family doctor. I believe you will find doctors want to help, and I found they understand confidentiality. If perhaps they do not feel comfortable about their ability to help you with drug dependency, they will refer you to someone who can. The important thing is to have a physical check-up and begin the healing process for problems caused by living in the fast lane.

Get Information—Call 800-COCAINE. This is a toll-free telephone referral and information service that is strictly confidential. You will receive immediate information on the nearest center to you.

Now—Turn to Chapter 12, "The Way to Escape," to learn how to avail yourself of the greatest power of change in the universe.

What Do You Think?

1. In spite of the cost, do you believe cocaine use is a problem in your area? Of the users you may know, do any sell drugs to support their habit?
2. What is the biggest danger in cocaine use? List several.
3. In thinking of the temporary effects of cocaine, why would it become so popular? Does cocaine fill a need temporarily in some lives?
4. Do most people think of the information presented on the danger of coke as a scare tactic rather than the truth? Is there enough evidence to support these claims of danger? Weighing the pleasures against the dangers, is it worth the risk?
5. Are teen-agers influenced by comments of famous comedians or songs by rock stars about the pleasure of cocaine?
6. If you were to try to convince someone not to try cocaine or to discontinue using it, what would be some options you could offer them to the pleasures of cocaine? What can you as an individual do to help? What about as a group?

4.

The Chemical Curtain: LSD, PCP (Angel Dust), STP, and Others

WE WILL FIRST EXAMINE THE VARIous hallucinogens, which are also called psychedelics. As the name suggests, these drugs cause hallucinations. They provoke changes in the user's emotions, self-awareness, and reasoning abilities. They distort or intensify the user's perception of time and space, which is why a user will speak of being able to "see sounds" or "hear colors." These psychedelic experiences may be minimal or overwhelming, depending upon the dosage, its strength, the personality of the user, the user's experience with the drug, and even the environment in which the drug is taken. The psychedelic drugs are mind-altering because of their direct action on the brain cells. The most frequently abused hallucinogens are LSD, DMT, mescaline, STP, peyote, psilocybin, PCP, and marijuana. These are the drugs that gained such notoriety in the 1960s because of their bizarre and unpredictable effects.

LSD

According to the National Institute of Mental Health, LSD is the most potent and best-studied psychedelic.

LSD is short for lysergic acid diethylamide, a relatively new drug. Lysergic acid comes from ergot, the fungus that spoils rye grain. For centuries, from Spain to Russia, the parasitic fungus ergot spoiled many a rye field during particularly wet summers. When through extreme hunger or ignorance the contaminated grain was eaten, gangrene of the extremities resulted. The condition was called "St. Anthony's Fire" because the blackened toes and fingers looked charred. Abortions, visual disturbances, and mental changes culminating in epidemics of madness also followed the eating of spoiled rye flour, according to records from the Middle Ages.

Ergot, the purple fungus *Claviceps purpurea*, is a veritable chemical factory. It contains a large number of active substances, including ergotine, which is used after childbirth to contract the uterus, and ergotamine, used for the treatment of migraine headaches. Ergot contains lysergic acid, which in itself is not hallucinogenic.

The substance was first converted to lysergic acid diethylamide (LSD) in 1938 by Swiss chemist Albert Hofman, who discovered its mind-altering properties when he accidentally inhaled or swallowed a minute amount in 1943.[1] It is ironic that in his search for a cure for migraine headaches he gave the world a headache of a different sort.

LSD exists in both liquid and powder form and is colorless, tasteless, and odorless. Many users put liquid LSD on sugar cubes, aspirin, crackers, and even bread. I used to put it on chewing gum and on pieces of blotter paper (hence the term "blotter acid"). It can also be put on postage stamps. A friend of mine was sentenced to jail for pushing drugs. I sent him letters with liquid LSD on the back of the postage stamps. He could take a trip and never leave the county jail.

One of the astonishing properties of LSD is the instant and lasting action caused by infinitesimal amounts. It is two hundred times stronger than cocaine. From one ounce, three hundred thousand adult doses can be obtained. Two pounds would disorder every person in New York City for eight hours. A dose of fifty to two hundred micrograms (no larger than the point of a pin) will put the drug user on a trip for eight to sixteen hours because the substance remains in the bloodstream and brain cells for at least that long. One drop of liquid LSD can make five hundred people high. LSD is also called LSD-25, "acid," "trip," "orange sunshine," "cubes," and "Lucy in the Sky with Diamonds."

LSD—Trip or Trap?

The subject of LSD is a very controversial one, mainly because of the drug's mind-altering properties. Some call LSD an hallucinogen because it causes hallucinations and temporary insanity. Others call it a psychedelic because it produces psychedelic experiences and induces states of self-transcendence and mystical unity. Because of this mystical state, many mistakenly call the LSD trip a "religious experience." Professor Timothy Leary, founder of the League for Spiritual Discovery and the Church of the Tree of Life in San Francisco, is one of those who taught that religious experience can be found through mind-altering drugs.

However, having experienced trips on LSD and many other hallucinogens and having since been reborn in Jesus Christ, I can say there is absolutely no comparison between the two. To say that they are the same is like saying an artificial pearl is the best pearl and thereby denying oneself the joy of owning the real thing. This League for Spiritual Discovery should have been named "The League for Self-Destruction."

Many say LSD destroys, disrupts, and disorganizes mental activity, while others say it expands the mind and organizes it. I know from personal experience, as well as from listening to hundreds of teens on trips, that it does not expand the mind or make one more creative. In fact, it usually has just the opposite effect. Virtually every person I try to help through an LSD trip becomes fearful that he is losing his mind or going crazy. After he has crashed (come down), there is no visual proof of the drug's alleged creative ability. In fact, LSD reduces motivation to work at anything. In reality, "turning on" is the same as "dropping out."

In *The Master Game*, Robert DeRopp comments on Baudelaire's hunger of soul and suggests that within the psyche of man are secret rooms, vast chambers full of treasure with windows looking out on eternity and infinity. Man rarely enters these rooms. They are locked, and man has lost the key. He lives habitually in the lowest, dreariest, darkest part of inner habitation.

DeRopp raises the question: "Do psychedelics offer the key to these locked rooms, or do they constitute a form of spiritual burglary that carries its own hazards and penalties?"[2] From my own experience and my observation of thousands who have been damaged or destroyed by psychedelics, I vote that they constitute spiritual burglary.

DeRopp also states that a drug experience might

give a glimpse of a higher state of consciousness, but admits that psychedelics cannot enable the user to raise his level of consciousness, no matter how often they are used. Continued use carries its own penalty of irreparable depletion of the spiritual substance needed for real inner work and total loss of an individual's developmental capacity.[3]

In trying to understand why teens would use a drug like LSD, please remember that it does produce a sensational high. Empty, bored teens are after thrills, so if LSD did not produce a super high, it never would have become so popular.

LSD's unpredictability is its greatest drawback. Although one trip might be exciting and enlightening, the next trip may be terrifying. Trying to describe an LSD trip is impossible; the intensity cannot be put down on paper. It is no wonder that those who use LSD regularly perceive it as a powerful and forceful drug; the effects are not easily forgotten. (It is interesting to note that while writing this book I could hardly remember good experiences I had while high on other drugs; but seven years later, the bad LSD trips are easily remembered.)

The effects of LSD are so strong that there is little desire to take it more than once a week; even among "acid heads," twice a week is about the limit. Because of the fear of a bad trip, many LSD users will not take the drug except in controlled settings.

LSD is known to cause depression, anxiety, and even psychotic breaks with reality that may last for a few days or even years. It can also induce tremendous panic or paranoia that can lead to injury or death. While intoxicated, the user may feel omniscient and indestructible and believe he can fly or walk on water. Although the user does not develop physical dependence (addiction), he may develop psychological dependence (habituation).

Another harmful effect of the drug is flashbacks. Those who frequently use LSD may experience recurrences of some features of an LSD trip months after the last dose. Because these flashbacks are often severe and sometimes fatal, there has been much research to determine their cause. The current theories suggest:

1. That the trips are *psychosomatic* recurrences without the drug's presence. This is something like a conditioned reflex based on previous reactions to the drug. (This theory should be accepted with great reservation, if at all, since the repeat trips are often much more severe than the "normal" trips these recurrences are supposed to reflect.)
2. That the repeat trips are *physically* induced and result from previous drug damage, again, without the drug being present. (With merit, this theory enjoys the support of many recent studies that agree with the notion that LSD does permanent damage to nerve endings. Reacting like an electrical circuit, the damaged nervous system seems to function normally until overloaded, then severe disorder and chaos follow.)
3. That the repeat trips are both *physically* and *mentally* induced. The drug is retained (stored) within the body to be released at some later time when triggered by a combination of physical/mental pressures. (This notion easily accounts for the combined physical/mental symptoms of many "flashback" victims.) It is also highly logical that the body could retain the drug, isolate the drug, and thereby protect itself from the drug, yet under certain conditions be unable to confine it. The drug stockpile would then be released into a system of low resistance (due to abstinence from the drug). The reaction would be likened to fifty or one hundred overdoses, which is exactly what often seems to take place.[4]

The American Medical Association warns that while on LSD or during a flashback, a person may believe he possesses supernatural powers, which may lead him to take chances with disastrous results. Many users have committed suicide, and other confess that during trips they have had suicidal tendencies. Moreover, even if a user quits the drug, it may not quit him.

LSD is made by back-street chemists in what are called "kitchens" or "labs." Since the substance is illegal, the pushers sometimes sell LSD of untested purity. These back-alley labs produce psychedelics in capsule, tablet, powder, and liquid forms. At almost every rock concert I have attended, pushers have been patrolling the parking lots on foot and in cars, trying to sell their homemade psychedelics. It is amazing that young people will buy pills from strangers and use them without knowing the quality, strength, or possible effects of these drugs.

It is imperative to remember that all synthetic psychedelics are made and sold by street chemists and street dealers, for it is illegal for any drug company to make them in America. Most home chemists are generally careless, unsanitary, and not at all exact. Therefore, you never know how strong or pure the drug is. The dealer may say this pill is strong enough for two people when it is actually strong enough for four, or he may tell you it is a little weak to get you to buy more. If it is weak, it will only give a nervous "buzz," and no one will be high, only disoriented. If it is too strong, it may cause a bad trip.

Often a batch of LSD comes out poor and must be doctored. The dealer who laces inadequate LSD with PCP (an animal tranquilizer) to increase its effects may tell the buyer it is actually organic mescaline or psilocybin. Remember, the dealer isn't as interested in turning people on as he is making money. If the chemist makes a mistake in a batch of LSD, he doesn't throw the batch away. Rather than lose money, he will sell it to a dealer under a different name; the dealer in turn sells it to teens on the street who don't know any better and who obviously don't care. Chemists also add belladonna, lysergic waste materials left over from the synthesis, speed, and PCP to stretch the volume of the drug and increase profits. When mixed with LSD, this "street garbage" greatly increases the chances of bad trips.

While the psychological dangers of LSD and other hallucinogens are well known, there is still a great deal to be learned about possible damage to the chromosomes and the reproductive systems of users. According to the National Clearing House for Drug Abuse, the Texas State Program on Drug Abuse, and the Special Action Office for Drug Abuse Prevention of the Executive Office of the President, because of limited research, no conclusive link can be found between LSD and chromosomal breaks or birth defects.

A number of investigators have been studying the effects of LSD on chromosomes, the microscopic threads of matter in the nucleus of every cell that carry genetic, or hereditary, characteristics and guide reproduction. While some scientists have tested LSD in labs and found it to cause chromosomal changes in animals and man, other equally capable scientists have found no such changes. Whether LSD can cause birth defects remains an open question; further studies are underway.

Nevertheless, until all the research is in, it is dangerous and foolish to swallow or inject anything that could severely harm the body processes. Medical authorities warn that LSD must be considered a definite risk, and women, particularly those of child-bearing age, are urged to refrain from using it. The Do It Now Foundation has published a helpful publication entitled *Chemical Use and Abuse of the Female Reproductive System* that reports the following:

It is believed by some researchers that pregnant women who use LSD have a much higher rate of miscarriage than non-users. There is also evidence that LSD is associated with the rupture or separation of the membranes in the placenta, which may account for the high miscarriage rate and the few infant deformities that have been reported.[5]

Obviously, this warrants further investigation. You can obtain this book by writing your state's clearing office on drug abuse prevention. This presence of other trash ingredients in the hallucinogens make it impossible to tell just what causes the damage or danger. In the words of Dr. Lindsay Curtis, "LSD isn't a trip; it is a trap."

MESCALINE AND PEYOTE

Mescaline and peyote are both made from a small, gray-green cactus that grows in northeastern Mexico and near the Rio Grande Valley of Texas. Peyote is the name of the cactus plant, and mescaline is the chemical derived from the buttons, the part that grows above the ground. This plant has been used for centuries by various Indian tribes of Central America (Aztecs and Mayas) and of the southwestern part of the United States (Comanches). The buttons are cut or sliced, then dried and ground into powder. Mescaline has a bitter taste when taken orally, which is the reason it is usually mixed with such liquids as tea, coffee, or orange juice.

A dose of mescaline will cause hallucinations approximately one hour later, and the trip will last from five to ten hours, possibly as long as eighteen hours. Synthetic mescaline (which is almost never available) is found as powder and put in capsules or tablets. The mescaline high includes LSD-type effects: sensation of weightlessness, euphoria, hallucinations, a trance-like state, hyperactivity, nausea, and dilation of the pupils.

Peyote and mescaline are not addictive, but can cause psychological dependence (habituation). In high-school assembly programs I am often asked, "What is wrong with taking an organic drug like mescaline or peyote for a 'mild' high?"

These are the risks involved: First of all, it is difficult to find a pure dose of the drug. There are eleven known alkaloids in the peyote cactus; most of them are undesirable and can trigger bad trips. They cause fever, vomiting, headache, cramps, and lower the blood pressure. Second, genuine mescaline can rarely be found. The chemical is expensive to process, and the dosage required for a satisfactory trip must be large. For example, one dose of pure mescaline would have to be larger than an Alka-Seltzer tablet, would have to cost at least twenty dollars, and would be bitter. In the third place, when a batch of acid (LSD) comes out wrong—too weak or too strong— the dealer often laces it with trash chemicals and sells it as mescaline.

PSILOCYBIN

Psilocybin is found in a certain type of mushroom grown in Mexico that, like peyote, has been used in Indian religious rites for centuries. Psilocybin is chemically related to LSD and DMT. The effects are basically the same as mescaline's, except that psilocybin requires a smaller dose and lasts for around six hours. It is found in crystal, liquid, or powder forms. The powder and liquid are sometimes mixed with Kool-Aid or punch at parties (hence the name "Electric Kool-Aid Acid"). Psilocybin may cause the user to feel relaxed, to experience hallucinations, dizziness, vomiting, paranoia, stomach pains and cramps, or to fall into a drunk-like trance. I have often found in counseling those on psilocybin trips that they feel as though they may die.

THC

THC is the active, mind-affecting ingredient in marijuana. First synthesized in 1966, it can be sold in tablets or capsules. The Do It Now Foundation, in cooperation with the University of California and certain pharmacy schools, has conducted street evaluation programs in the eastern United States, Canada, and Europe. All investigators report that after five years of testing street drugs, no one has ever been able to find one real, pure dose of THC. The reason is that THC is even harder and more expensive to manufacture than mescaline or psilocybin. Instead, the animal tranquilizer PCP is being sold as THC.

PCP (ANGEL DUST)

PCP is, I feel, the most dangerous street drug to come along since heroin and LSD. Although it is an entirely new psychoactive drug, I have placed it in the hallucinogen category because it does have hallucinogenic properties. PCP is a veterinary anesthetic (phencyclidine) sold under the trade name "Sernyl." It was originally manufactured legally by Parke, Davis and Company in 1956 as a surgical anesthetic. The company discontinued its use on humans in 1965 because it was found to be too dangerous. One out of every three patients woke up screaming, suffering from temporary insanity. It then became a legal animal tranquilizer. But since it is so potent, it must be cut with other drugs, because the side effects are too dangerous even for animals.

Many street chemists still make it because it is cheap and easy to make. The drug can be manufactured by anyone with a minimal knowledge of chemistry and a few pieces of equipment. From the seller's viewpoint, the profits are high, and since the drug can be manufactured in the back alley or bathroom, it is virtually impossible for law-enforcement agencies to locate the producer. Even if he is caught, the penalty is not much of a deterrent. In thirty-six hours, eleven chemicals, costing approximately $500, can be made into Angel Dust worth at least $200,000.

Back-street chemists mix PCP with LSD or sell it alone as THC, mescaline, or psilocybin. Most people think these are softer, milder drugs, making PCP easier to sell when doctored up. This is where drug education can help. The majority of teens believe LSD is a bad drug and PCP is mild, perhaps a bit heavier than grass.

PCP is a white crystalline powder and can be smoked, injected, or taken as a liquid, tablet, or capsule. It is also used in combination with other drugs. For example, marijuana is often soaked in it. PCP, which first appeared as "angel dust," was sprinkled on parsley, mint leaves, or marijuana, and then smoked. Probably more bad trips are caused by

PCP than by any other street drug. Those young people who use the drug regularly may never be normal again.

The effects can be compared to LSD's. PCP affects the central nervous system, causing the loss of all feeling in arms and legs. As an animal tranquilizer, it can knock out an elephant. It distorts the senses to the point of numbness and its users compare the effect to no feeling at all—a living death. It's been called by its users a "state of nothingness." It causes physical disorders such as double vision, dizziness, vomiting, and even convulsive seizures. It also causes memory loss, personality change, severe depression, and suicidal and homicidal tendencies. PCP is frightening enough alone; imagine its effects when mixed with LSD.

Unfortunately, it is easy for the novice chemist to err in making PCP. If not concocted exactly, the drug causes violent convulsions and the coughing up of blood, and sends many to the hospital. I wish I could tell you that the chemists are careful, that they are people of "love" who like to turn on, and that we are all brothers and sisters; *but* it just ain't so. The chemist sells drugs to the dealer, who must rely on what the chemist tells him.

Also, please remember that PCP is a tranquilizer or barbiturate. Often when someone has a bad trip (a common occurrence with PCP), a friend will give him a tranquilizer. This is dangerous, for if the user unknowingly has taken PCP under another name or mixed with LSD, he will overdose, and no one will understand why.

Federal officials estimate that at least seven million people have tried PCP. It has become third in popularity, after booze and grass. Most users are age twelve to twenty-five, with the average age of first use being fourteen. Alarmingly, PCP is now being taken by children as young as nine. Karst J. Besteman, acting director of the National Institute on Drug Abuse, said, "In 1976 alone PCP sent four thousand of its users to hospital emergency rooms. It took over one hundred lives and triggered untold numbers of strange suicidal and homicidal acts. One dose can last for months, and the problem is worsening." In Florida, a young man had a hallucination in which he saw a black cloud attacking an elderly woman. He ran to her defense and began attacking the cloud with a knife. He then took her car and drove halfway across the nation. He was stopped for speeding then arrested for a grotesque murder he doesn't remember committing.

In another highly publicized case in California, a man walked into a house and began attacking a pregnant woman. He was distracted by a crying baby, whom he stabbed to death. He returned to the young mother, who survived the attack but lost the baby she was carrying. This young man still has no recollection of what he did. Robert Blake of the old TV program, "Baretta," made a commercial regarding PCP: "Don't go near it. It's a rattlesnake; it will kill you." Recently there was a newspaper account of a young girl high on angel dust who ate several of her fingers. This is not to mention the accidents and blindness caused by PCP use.

PCP holds its users in a strong psychological grip. It often induces a state of depression, causing the user to start all over again on another PCP trip. PCP creates a Dr. Jekyll/Mr. Hyde who later has no memory of his actions while on the drug. It is both a mind high and a body high, loosening inhibitions.

PCP is sold on the street under seventy or eighty names, including "angel dust," "super brass," "mist," "tic tac," "peace pill," "hog," "cosmos," "rocket fuel," "crystal," "THC," "cannabinol," "dust," "duster," "sherman," "sher," "KW," and "sheets." In light of the dangerous effects of PCP, I move we change the name from angel dust to "demon dust."

STP

STP (DOM—dimethoxymethylamphetamine) first appeared on the psychedelic scene in spring of 1967. Articles in the underground newspapers promoted its use, claiming that STP is a "megahallucinogen," "one hundred times more powerful than LSD." The name itself is ironic: "scientifically treated petroleum," also called "serenity, tranquility, and peace." However, STP produces just the opposite effects in its users: nausea, tremors, delirium, and even convulsions. It has produced an unusually large number of bad trips. It is found in various colors and is available as a liquid or in tablets.

OTHER PSYCHEDELICS

DMT (dimethyltryptamine), known as the "businessman's trip," is an easily manufactured product and can be smoked, snuffed, or injected, but its popularity has waned. Its effects are very intense and brief in duration and too frightening and unpleasant for many.

MDA is a popular psychedelic drug made from a speed-based derivative. One reason for its popularity is that it induces fewer audiovisual distortions and more introspection. Many users, desiring hallucinations, take too large a dose, and at high doses it has caused serious physical reactions requiring medical treatment.

Other psychedelic drugs on the scene are PMA, morning glory seeds, nutmeg, and jimson weed.

SNIFFING SOLVENTS

Solvents are substances which were never meant to be inhaled by man, as they contain dangerous chemicals. It is hard to believe that many teen-aged boys and girls are actually getting high sniffing glue, household cement, paint thinner, gasoline, cleaning fluid, fingernail polish remover, and aerosols. Solvents can be poured into plastic bags or soaked into rags and inhaled or sniffed. This practice has taken the lives of many young people by subsequently causing cardiac arrest.

Solvent-sniffing results in a high lasting anywhere from five minutes to an hour. This high includes drunkenness, confusion, loosening of inhibitions, and an elevated mood. The user becomes very clumsy, dizzy, and drowsy. I have seen many teens high on solvents, walking around like zombies, periodically convulsed by attacks of uncontrollable laughter.

The results are frightening: Consider the deaths caused by heart attack, asphyxiation, and lead poisoning. It is believed that acute brain damage, liver and kidney damage, bone marrow damage, and blood abnormalities result from inhalation of solvents. We do know that the practice causes temporary liver and kidney damage, gastritis, jaundice, and peptic ulcers.

What Do You Think?

1. What is an LSD flashback? What are the real dangers behind a flashback and can it be avoided?
2. At one time PCP was a legal drug used for a specific purpose. What was it?
3. Who manufactures LSD and PCP? Is it the same recipe and same effect each time? Because a person can handle one or two trips, does it mean he will never have a bad trip?
4. Solvents are simple to come by, inexpensive to purchase, and quick and easy to use. Are they dangerous if used sparingly or only if used too often in heavy doses?
5. Many teens have this idea: "As long as I don't hurt anyone else, as long as I am the only person involved, I should be able to do drugs because my body is mine and what I do with it is my own business."
   a. Is it possible to use drugs and only affect yourself? Why?
   b. Who does your body belong to? Is your right the only one to be considered?

5.

The Elevator Drugs: Going Up and Down

BASICALLY THERE ARE THREE TYPES of pills subject to abuse: amphetamines (stimulants, uppers); barbiturates (depressants, downers); and tranquilizers. It is helpful to remember that all am phetamines speed up the metabolism and all barbiturates and tranquilizers slow it down.

There are millions—a number of them adults—hiding behind pills. They take pills to pep up and pills to calm down; pills to gain weight and pills to lose weight; pills to find life and pills to escape life. It's no wonder street kids call this a "yo-yo" existence.

STIMULANTS—GOING UP?

Stimulants are drugs, usually amphetamines, that act to stimulate the central nervous system. Until recently, stimulants were widely prescribed by doctors for treatment of depression, obesity, and narcolepsy (sleepiness), as well as to promote wakefulness and to combat fatigue. Stimulants have had wide non-medical use by students cramming for final exams, by truck drivers and salesmen driving long distances, and even by night-shift workers and athletes who desire extra energy.

The most commonly known stimulants are amphetamines, methamphetamine, cocaine, caffeine, ritalin, and nicotine. Stimulants are known by various street names: "uppers," "speed," "meth," "crystal," "pep pills," "co-pilots," "wake-ups," "bennies," "footballs," "dexies," "diet pills," and others. The slang names are frequently derived from the shapes and colors of the capsules or tablets and from their effects. The tablets or capsules are round or heart-shaped and are either blue, yellow, pink, rose-colored, green, or orange.

Approximately 50 percent of almost fifteen billion amphetamine tablets and pills produced in the United States yearly are sold illegally on the street and in the schools for just a few dollars. Much of the other 50 percent obtained legally are used abusively. Some users obtain the drugs by fraud—stealing doctors' prescription pads and forging prescriptions (Who can read a doctor's signature?). Many teens go so far as to rob pharmacies. Stimulants are made illegally in secret laboratories.

The Do It Now Research Center reports that most of the amphetamines on the streets are in pill forms called "white crosses" or "mini-whites." The center has tested many of the white crosses at different times and from different places and has found that they vary each time in strength and quality. This is dangerous. On one occasion a pill might be very weak so that the user increases his dosage the next time; if the pills in the second dosage turn out to be potent (full of speed), then the user ends up in the hospital.

Speed may be swallowed, inhaled, snorted, or injected through a needle. Experienced users often take the pill or powder from the capsule, dissolve it in a small amount of water, and inject the fluid into a vein. This is a serious step, because it marks the move from experimentation to serious abuse. Intravenous use is extremely dangerous; it involves all the complications of needle contamination (hepatitis and infection), and it can increase the chance of death from overdose. It also puts damaging impurities into the body. An injection of the drug directly into the vein (shooting up) greatly increases the immediacy and intensity of the effect. This is called a "rush." Speed users abuse the drug in "runs" or "sprees"; they will speed for days or even a week. But what goes up must come down; after the run the user will "crash." This results in depression, irritability, confusion, delirium, and fatigue, so the user once again goes on the "run."

*Methamphetamine—(Diet pills until injected—
then "speed")*

Methamphetamine is chemically related to amphetamine, but it has more central nervous system activity. Methamphetamine is injected directly into the veins. This was the drug that made my life hell off and on for several years. This drug is called "speed" (because of the rush received when it is injected), "crystal," or "meth," and its abuse is more widespread than ever before. The user needs to shoot up several times a day. There is not a true addiction, but the user does develop a tolerance and requires larger and larger doses to feel the effects of the drug. Speed becomes an emotional crutch, and the high is so great that it is difficult to rehabilitate a "speed freak."

Speed withdrawal produces marked psychological changes, including a tremendous craving for the drug, overwhelming depression, and fatigue so severe it may provoke suicide. In response to the feelings of weakness, fatigue, and depression, the amphetamine user will begin the cycle again.

Speed users are inconsistent people because their ups and downs are so unpredictable. One day I was friendly and kind; the next, I was irritable and cross. I would make promises one day and have no recollection of them the next. It was very upsetting for those around me (teachers, girl friends, buddies, and parents), because most had no idea what was going on. Few were willing to bear the burden of our relationship.

W. R. Spence coined the slogan, "Speed kills...don't meth around," which is certainly true. Speed prevents the body from eating and sleeping, its two most necessary functions. Long-term speeding is like a running a car day and night without gas or oil—it can't be done. Speed freaks, having neither eaten nor slept properly for weeks or months, are always subject to maladies such as viruses and infections. Speed also causes heart, liver, and brain damage, as well as complete exhaustion.

Speed kills the mind. Once hooked on the drug, a person cannot live without it. He becomes very unhappy, pities himself, and becomes angry with others easily. To function in society he depends on his crutch and strength—the drug.

Speed also causes paranoia; during a run the user may imagine that he sees images other than himself in a mirror. He may exhibit nervous habits such as muscle twitches, irritability, babbling, suspiciousness, and violence. Speed damages the brain to the point that a speed freak may forget simple words he has known for years.

SEDATIVES—GOING DOWN?

The sedatives belong to a large family of drugs that relax the central nervous system, just the opposite of what stimulants do. The family includes sedatives, barbiturates, and depressants. All produce a drowsiness and drunkenness by depressing the normal physical functions of the body. The street name for sedatives is "downers," and the best known are barbiturates.

Barbiturates are made from barbituric acid, which was first produced in 1846. Barbiturates usually appear as capsules.

The Effects

The effects of the downer depend on several variables: the chemistry of the drug, the physical and psychological makeup of the person taking it, the social setting in which the drug is taken, and even the means by which it is taken. Barbiturates usually make a person drowsy, relax muscles, cause loss of inhibitions, and promote euphoria (a sense of well-being). The effects are like those of drunkenness, except there is little sickness, no booze smell or breath odor and the drug is much cheaper than alcohol—only twenty-five to fifty cents per pill. Barbiturates often are used by teen-agers to make their dates more cooperative and sexually vulnerable.

Barbiturates are worse than speed (methamphetamine) or smack (heroin), because they can cause brain damage by cutting down the amount of oxygen necessary to the brain cells. For decades, overdosing on sleeping pills has been a popular form of suicide. Death is caused by respiratory depression and, finally, cardiac arrest.

It is a well-known fact on the streets that barbiturates are addictive. The Do It Now Research Center says barbiturates are the most addictive of all legal drugs and of most illegal ones. Even if only a few downers are taken on weekends, the first weekend without them will bring sickness. Many people take barbiturates to go to sleep, but after repeated use sleep cannot come without them; the body needs increasingly higher doses to feel the effects of the drug.

Some drug experts believe that barbiturate addiction is more difficult to cure than narcotic addiction. If the barbiturates are stopped abruptly, withdrawal begins; the user suffers withdrawal sickness, including cramps, nausea, delirium, and convulsions that, in some cases, may cause death. This is why most drug counselors demand that withdrawal take place in a hospital over a period of days or weeks. It takes months for the body to return to normal, because heavy use of downers can cause irreparable damage to the kidneys and liver. Research clearly reveals that barbiturates are as addicting as heroin.

Please remember that barbiturate overdoses kill more users of legal and illegal drugs than any other type of overdose in America today. And alarmingly, they kill just as many adults as they do teen-agers. The search today seems to be for "awayness" and oblivion rather than for awareness and alertness.

POLY-DRUG ABUSE: THE MOST DEADLY GAME

Many people today mix drugs, especially barbiturates and alcohol. Among adults, the cocktail-and-sleeping-pill combination causes untold accidental suicides. Death occurs because it is easier for the liver to detoxify the alcohol than the barbiturates. The alcohol is given top priority, and the downers, which are supposed to travel through the circulatory system only one time, wait in line by traveling again and again through the circulatory system. The body reacts as if many times the actual dosage has been taken. The result is overdose.

Among teens, accidental suicides often occur when barbiturates are mixed with beer or wine. The most common barbiturate abused on the streets is Seconal. This comes in red capsules called "reds," "pinks," "red devils," "red birds," and "seggy" (after the trade name). Whenever you hear a teen saying he got "high" on reds, think of him as a beginner, because "low" is really the result.

Reds are not the only kind of barbiturate. Nembutals ("yellow jackets"—yellow capsules), Amytal ("blue heavens"—blue capsules), and Tuinal ("rainbows," "double-trouble"—red and blue capsules) are others.

Beware the mixture of wine or beer with angel dust, angel hair, or LSD because many of these drugs are cut with PCP. Mixture with alcohol can cause unexpected overdose. Many school-agers are so desperately seeking thrills and kicks that they remove pills from the medicine cabinet at home, place the pills in a bowl, and then take several of their favorite-colored pills. This is often called "rainbow chasing" or "fruit salad."

Needless to say, a number of bad trips result from the mixing of drugs. "One plus one equals three" in poly-drug use. When combined, each drug multiplies the effect of the other.

Tranquilizers

Tranquilizers are drugs that diminish anxiety. Like sedatives, they cause drowsiness and sleep. Unlike downers and uppers, which have only a single basic ingredient, different tranquilizers have different ingredients that affect different parts of the body. Some may work on parts of the brain, while others work on the central nervous system, and others relax the muscles.

The most commonly used tranquilizers today are Valium, Librium, Quaaludes, Sopors, and Thorazine.

Valium and Librium are commercial names for two of the three most doctor-prescribed drugs in America. These are "anti-anxiety" pills, mild tranquilizers used to relieve tension without causing sleep. When used in large doses, they can cause a psychological dependence just like barbiturates. The most frequent abusers of these drugs are middle-class adults who get hooked without realizing it. *Don't* drop these and drink—the combination is lethal. Remember, if you haven't taken many barbiturates before, you can overdose on four to eight capsules.

My wife and I had business dealings on several occasions with a good-looking, well-dressed woman. She was a nice person, but we noticed that her personality and mood changed without warning. We never really gave it much thought until later, when we discovered her problem. This middle-class professional woman, a mother, wife, and Christian, had become a drug addict. First there were tranquilizers and sleeping pills to calm the tensions of the day, and then there were diet pills to curb the appetite. Soon the diet pills gave energy, and the tranquilizers calmed and gave sleep. She found she could renew her prescriptions at most drug stores, no questions asked. And then, one day she ran out unexpectedly, and the stores were closed. She could not understand the sickness and craving, the nervousness and cramps that followed. Finally she was forced to accept the truth—she had become an addict. Unintentionally, yes. Unsuspectingly, yes. But an addict, nevertheless. It happens this way to thousands.

In the early seventies, methaqualone (known as Quaaludes and Sopors) was the blue-chip stock of both licit and illicit drug industries. It was so plentiful that it caused a great deal of damage in colleges and high schools; the manufacturers gave it the "fun aspirin" image and promoted it as completely safe and non-addictive. The drug relaxes the user so much that walking straight and talking clearly become a chore. Methaqualone lightens the head, induces a warm and friendly feeling, and relaxes inhibitions; this is why many attribute aphrodisiac properties to it. Current heavy street use has shown it to be very addictive and dangerous and should only be done under medical supervision. Combination with alcohol results in overdose.

What Do You Think?

1. Name at least three ways speed use can begin "innocently." How does it then develop to continued and greater use?
2. The use of speed deprives the user of two basic, essential needs for the body. Name these needs and the effects of trying to live without them both as an occasional or as a regular speed user.
3. Speed is often used in the beginning to "speed

up" life, but when the user is strung out, he often turns to other drugs to "slow down." What type of drugs are then used? What is the danger in combining the two?

4. Are barbiturates addicting? What is the most common cause of barbiturate addiction? How long does it take to get addicted—the first time, the third, the twentieth?

5. Do you think users of speed and downers start their use knowing they will be hooked? Does anyone actually set out to be a statistic? How does it happen?

6. Is there any drug that can be safely mixed with alcohol?

6.

The Enslaving Narcotics

THE WORD "NARCOTIC" (FROM THE Greek *narkotikos*, "benumbing") refers generally to opium and to pain-killing drugs derived from opium.

Opium is the milky juice of the unripe pods of the poppy. This poppy juice is dried to form a brown, gummy material. The opium family includes opium, morphine, and heroin.

OPIUM

Opium has been used recreationally since at least 300 B.C. The famous Greek poet Homer called it "the potent destroyer of grief." Homer attributed its discovery to the Egyptians, who in turn say they learned about it from the peasants of Asia Minor, who may have used it thousands of years before its addictive ability was discovered. While visiting Asia, I learned that many of the peasants are addicted. Their supply is plentiful, and their simple lifestyle does not require a clear, rational mind or even mental alertness, so they do not realize their addiction to opium. The opium-induced high is a dreamy, lazy state which serves as an escape from the monotonous misery of daily existence. As far as we can tell, opium has been labeled addictive and harmful since 300 B.C., when the Greek physican Erasistratus so labeled it.

First introduced in the East as a cure for dysentery and for the prevention of malaria, opium was providing relief from physical and mental pain throughout Asia by the 1700s. The opium plague was such that by 1729 the Emperor Yung Cheng prohibited the sale and use of opium and even sought to close the opium dens. Needless to say, this decree was powerless. Eventually, the banning of opium cultivation and the importing of foreign opium led to the Opium Wars between England and China for three long years. History tells us that almost half of the adult male population in mainland China was addicted to opium by the 1900s.

The opium plague also swept Europe and England. Opium addicts were found not only among the peasants of Asia, but also in England's upper middle class. Those who study English literature tell us of the many fine writers who were disciples of the god of opium. Among the most familiar was Thomas DeQuincy, who wrote "Confessions of an English Opium Eater," originally published in 1821. He said:

> Happiness might now be bought for a penny and
> carried in your waist coat pocket.
> Portable ecstasies might be had in a bottle
> and peace of mind sent by the mail.

Other famous opium devotees were Samuel Taylor Coleridge, Edgar Allan Poe, and Elizabeth Barrett Browning.

Morphine, which is derived from opium, was administered to thousands of the Civil War wounded to relieve pain, and over one million U.S. opium addicts were thereby created.

At least three lessons can be learned from the

history of opiate use. First, it may take a long time before the adverse effects of a drug become apparent. The addictive potential of opium was not known for hundreds of years. When morphine became available in the 1850s, it was unwittingly used to cure opium dependence. Heroin later was introduced to cure those addicted to morphine.

Second, a change in the cultural setting or in the manner in which the drug is taken causes entirely new problems. Smoking a pipeful of opium on a remote farm in Asia is hardly comparable to shooting up heroin in a thriving metropolis.

Third, a drug fad adopted from the ghetto by middle- or upper-class intellectuals is likely to be a poor choice. Thus, the intelligentsia is not always that intelligent.

In reviewing the brief history of opium and its derivatives I have attempted to show a parallel to the recent popularization of psychedelic and other mind- and mood-altering drugs in America. The drug problem is blamed on difficult, depressing, disillusioning times. Now, as at other times and places in the past, people feel alienated and disenchanted with the prevailing social system. Mind-altering drugs like opium relieve pain and anxiety and produce a sense of euphoria. But continued use results in addiction.

MORPHINE

Morphine is derived from opium. This much-abused painkiller is roughly ten percent opium. It was discovered in 1805, and the physical addiction was once called "soldier's sickness." Morphine is more addictive than opium, and the addiction occurs after several weeks of daily use. Morphine is called "white stuff," "M," "hard stuff," "Unkie," and "Miss Emma" on the streets. When taken, it produces a dreamlike state with mental distortions, visual and physical impairment, and euphoria. Perhaps this is why this painkiller is named after the Greek god Morpheus, the god of dreams.

HEROIN

Heroin is another member of the opium family and is derived from morphine. In 1898, the Bayer Company in Germany isolated this "wonder drug" for pain and coughing. It was found to be two or three times more potent a painkiller than morphine and was used to relieve morphine addiction and withdrawal because it was not thought to be addictive. It was named Heroisch ("large and powerful"). Once again, it was years before scientists realized that heroin's addictive power was stronger than morphine's. Heroin is known on the streets as "H," "horse," "white stuff," "Harry," "joy powder," "smack," and "junk."

Heroin is a white, odorless, crystalline powder synthesized from morphine. Grain for grain, it is up to ten times more potent than morphine in its pharmacological effects. Heroin has no legal medical purpose in the United States, so the entire United States supply is imported from the Middle and Far East (Asia) and Mexico.

The quality of heroin varies. Only about 5 percent of the heroin sold is considered a safe buy. On the streets, heroin is invariably diluted with milk sugar, quinine, baking soda, and even talcum powder. Capsules or cellophane "decks" or "bags" may vary from 0 to 10 percent heroin and sell for about five to ten dollars. The material is not sterile and is cut with impurities and fillers by many successive dealers. At times heroin is very weak, but the addict may still derive psychological satisfaction from the street life and the ritual of the fix. Many are psychologically dependent on the needle itself, a situation called the "needle habit," in which one receives gratification from hustling narcotics and injecting himself.

Since almost all the terrible and horrifying reports about heroin are true, it seems incredible that people would use it in the first place. I believe people begin using heroin for at least two reasons.

First, some people refuse to listen to others, particularly to ministers, parents, or teachers. Teens would rather believe their friends. Anyone who tells you heroin is great is a rookie (a new user) or a pusher who needs to sell it. A habitual user knows it brings destruction. I wish it were possible for every teen to accompany me in the street ministry to see the hell-on-earth existence of the junkie. I wish teens would listen to stories of ex-junkies or visit junkies, who will tell them, "Addiction is the closest thing to hell itself."

Second, many teens feel there is not going to be much of a future. This attitude produces a "live-for-today" philosophy. "You only go around once, so grab all the gusto you can get," urges the commercial. Most think about that next high with no real concern for the future.

A teen looking for a high goes to his source or dealer and learns there are no more pills. "Why not try junk?" asks the pusher. I was afraid of needles, so I was told I could snort (inhale) heroin. I was fortunate not to follow the yellow brick road to addiction. (Snorting heroin can lead to addiction; it simply takes longer.) I did try "joy popping," which is to inject drugs just under the skin instead of into the vein. Fortunately, at this stage I was introduced to a Friend who changed my life.

Usually heroin is injected intravenously with a hypodermic needle; this is called "mainlining." The heroin is measured in a teaspoon, and water is added to dissolve it quickly. It is then "cooked," or heated, by a lighter, match, or candle. This liquid is drawn into a needle through a ball of cotton to strain out the impurities. Some sort of tourniquet (usually a belt or rope) is tightly applied to the arm to cause the veins to pop out so that it is easier to hit the vein with the needle. The first heroin injection usually brings sickness and vomiting. A doctor friend told me that the body immediately recognizes and tries to rid itself of the poison. After the sickness passes, the high—a warm, blissful feeling—comes on. So the rookie mainlines again, and then again. The testimony of most junkies I know is: "It started out to be just on Saturday nights, and soon on Friday and Saturday nights, and then on Thrusday, Friday, and Saturday nights, and on it went."

Very soon the rookie is an addict, even though most believe it could never happen to them. Once hooked, the body and mind require the heroin every day just to feel normal. If the body does not have its craving fulfilled, withdrawal sickness begins twelve to sixteen hours after the last fix. At first there is uncontrollable yawning, then the shakes, sweating, runny nose and eyes, vomiting, diarrhea, tremendous stomach cramps (that feel like someone inside is trying to tear his way out), backaches, muscle aches, and jerks (hence the term "kicking the habit"). Finally come the delusions and terrifying hallucinations. Many who try to quit give up the effort and desperately run for another fix. Little wonder many will do anything to avoid the hellish withdrawal sickness.

As tolerance to the drug develops, the "high" is generally lost and the addict requires heroin just to avoid withdrawal sickness. This tolerance develops so quickly that users soon find they must shoot up two or three times a day just to feel normal. Many addicts have habits that are quite expensive, ranging from thirty-five to one hundred dollars a day. This "monkey on the back" must be fed; if you become a junkie, you must be able to pay the pusher every day. This is part of the cause-and-effect relationship that leads junkies to become pushers. Like everything else, heroin is cheaper in volume. The more that is bought, the cheaper it is by the bag, or grain. Whatever is left over can be sold.

If the addict cannot sell enough to feed his habit, he must look for other ways to get the money. He soon learns to hustle in order to survive. He lies, cheats, steals, and even sells his body (prostitution) just to buy those white grains.

Society also has to pay for the rehabilitation of the addict. The female addict almost inevitably turns to prostitution on the streets; she has to "turn tricks" to get her money. She spends the hours from dusk to dawn shooting heroin and selling her favors. If she doesn't succumb to the hazards of heroin use, sooner or later she will succumb to the ravages of age. Unwanted, hideous in her own eyes, and dreading her days, she becomes a totally displaced person.

The greatest danger from heroin is overdose, since the potency of street drugs is never known until they are used. The average bag is 3 percent heroin. All of a sudden, some 10 percent stuff might come in, and no one knows it. Another danger is in never knowing where the junk comes from; Asian heroin is much different from brown Mexican junk and Middle East junk. To complicate the matter, heroin is mixed with many fillers.

If pure and germ-free heroin were available to the consumer, if the technique of injection assured complete sterility, and if tolerance did not develop, then most of the junkie's diseases could be avoided. But in real life none of these criteria are met, and therefore we see disastrous results from persistent heroin use.

There are many complications resulting from the use of contaminated drugs or needles. Any germs on the needle go directly into the blood, which is how the virus of serum hepatitis is transmitted. Many times junkies share their "works," and if one person has the virus, the whole gang gets it. Liver disease causes the infected person to turn yellow all over, even in the whites of his eyes. Addicts also are subject to tetanus, heart and lung abnormalities, ulcers, and abscesses. Babies born to addicted mothers may be born addicted.

This poem provides a vivid picture of heroin addiction:

So now, little man...
You have grown tired of grass,
LSD, acid, cocaine, and hash,
and someone pretending to be a true friend,
said: "I'll introduce you to Miss Heroin."

The Enslaving Narcotics

Well, honey, before you start fooling with me,
just let me inform you of how it will be.
For I will seduce you and make you my slave.
I have sent men much stronger than you to their
grave.

You think you could never become a disgrace
and end up addicted to poppy seed waste.

So you will start inhaling me one afternoon.
You'll take me into your arms very soon.

And once I have entered deep down
in your veins,
the craving will nearly drive you insane.

You will need lots of money, as you have been told,
for, darling, I am much more expensive than gold.

You'll swindle your mother, and just for a buck,
you'll turn into something vile and corrupt.

You'll mug and you'll steal for my narcotic charm
and feel contentment when I'm in your arms.

The day when you realize the monster you've grown,
you will solemnly promise to leave me alone.

If you think you have got the mystical knack,
then sweetie, just try getting me off your back.

The vomit, the cramps, your gut tied in a knot,
the jangling nerves screaming for just one more shot.

The hot chills, the cold sweat, the withdrawal pains,
can only be saved by my little white grains.

There is no other way and there's no need to look,
for deep down inside you will know you are hooked.

You will desperately run to the pusher and then,
you will welcome me back to your arms once again.

And when you return, just as I foretold,
I know you will give me your body and soul.

You will give up your morals, your conscience, your heart,
and you will be mine... until death do us part.

—Anonymous

METHADONE

So much attention has been given to methadone that some discussion is appropriate here. Methadone (Dolophine or Amidone commercially) is a synthetically produced narcotic used in the treatment of heroin addiction. Methadone acts to block the craving for heroin by relieving heroin's physical sickness. There are no kicks or highs, and it produces a cross-tolerance to heroin. There are several advantages to methadone. It can be taken orally (usually with orange juice) and work for more than twenty-four hours. It also allows the patient to drive, study, and work.

In reality, methadone treatment substitutes one form of addiction for another, like providing an alcoholic with beer instead of bourbon. Withdrawal from methadone still produces sickness. Pregnant women on methadone tend to deliver babies of low weight who must go through withdrawal.

People are always asking why it is so difficult to shut off the flow of heroin into the states. The problem is centuries old: "The love of money is the root of all evil..." (I Tim. 6:10). It is a matter of economics for the thousands of farmers who are growing those poppies in Burma, China, Egypt, India, Iran, Laos, Lebanon, Mexico, Syria, Thailand, and Turkey. According to the Texas State Program on Drug Abuse, a hundred kilograms of raw opium brings twenty-five thousand dollars to a farmer in Turkey. Resold on the streets as heroin, it brings as much as forty-four million dollars.

In an effort to halt this illegal importation, the United States Government paid Turkey thirty-five million dollars in 1972 to discontinue its production of poppy flowers. But in mid-1974, the Turkish government nullified the agreement and announced the poppies would again bloom. Heroin is big business.

What Do You Think?

1. Why would a teen-ager listen to the horrors of the addiction of heroin—the sickness, the pain, the emotional upheaval, the moral decay—and also listen to the claims of joy of heroin by pushers and users, and then go ahead and experiment with the drug?
2. Read the poem on heroin addiction on pages 98-100. Count the number of problems and dangers listed. Now list some of the pleasures of heroin claimed by users. How does the scale balance out?
3. Is it possible to be an "occasional" heroin user? What is the difference between the person who "occasionally" uses drugs and the person who never uses them? Describe the difference in the attitude toward life, in obeying the laws of the land, in the guidelines used in goal and decision making for the future.

4. The Bible does not specifically mention the name of the drug heroin. How, then, can we go about determining how things not specifically named as right or wrong in the Bible affect the Christian life?

7.

Recognizing Symptoms of Drug Abuse

THE OLD SAYING, "ROME WASN'T built in a day," is appropos of drug abuse. Addicts aren't made in a day. They don't just arrive; rather, they travel down a long, well-marked road. They are out of step, and they can be identified by alert and concerned adults.

It is imperative to remember that the effect of the drug on the user involves physical and psychological factors. The physical factors include the type of alcohol or the potency of the drug, how much and how fast the alcohol has been drunk, or the dosage of the drug. Whether the user has a full or empty stomach at the time of taking the drug determines the rate of absorption into the bloodstream and, thus, the drug's effect.

The psychological factors that vary the effects include the personality, mood, and attitude of the user. If the user is extremely upset (angry or sad), his high will be different than if he is in a pleasant mood. The expectations of the user and his previous drug experience also will determine the effects of the drug.

LSD—The most obvious physical reaction is a dilation of the pupils, because the user's eyes become very sensitive to light. A trip lasts anywhere from eight to sixteen hours, during which time the user is restless and unable to sleep. There is an increase in the heart rate, blood pressure, blood sugar, and temperature. Many times the user will experience "goose bumps," profuse perspiration, and even nausea. LSD may also cause hyperventilation (excessive and rapid breathing in deep, gulping breaths) and induce tremors (uncontrollable shaking and quivering of the whole body or limbs). If an unusually large quantity is taken, LSD may cause convulsions.

While high, the user experiences extreme changes of mood and loses control of normal thought processes. His moods may range from hilarity to uncontrollable exhilaration to withdrawal from reality; he may experience delusions or hallucinations. He may believe he cannot be harmed, or become paranoid and panic, depending on his emotional state at the time of taking the drug. If a teen is an experienced user, he will be able to handle these reactions, whereas many a novice will believe he is going insane.

The cause-and-effect relationship between LSD and emotional disturbance has not been established. We know that when a person has suffered from emotional disturbance before the use of a chemical, the drug may trigger a complete emotional breakdown. The LSD experience can add to existing neuroses and character disorders.

Most teens avoid contact with straights while tripping; most also try to hide the use of drugs from their parents. The real danger of LSD is the already-mentioned flashback, which can occur without warning weeks and months after the last dose of the drug. After a trip a user may exhibit acute anxiety and depression for a day or so.

Mescaline—This high involves a dreamlike trance and an exaggerated sense of joy and well-being. As with LSD, perception is affected, a condition that can last up to eighteen hours. Mescaline has been known to cause vomiting and headaches, and it lowers the blood pressure and heart rate.

Psilocybin—The effects are very similar to LSD's but last a shorter time. There is an inability to concentrate and the user may feel relaxed and detached. Bad side-effects include a flu-like nausea, dizziness, and tremors, accompanied by anxiety. A trip lasts six hours at the most.

STP—Dilation of the pupils, nausea, confusion, and sweating are the results of STP use—effects similar to those caused by LSD. A trip lasts eight to ten hours.

PCP (angel dust)—This drug has already been dealt with in detail. It causes a high degree of agitation, anxiety, and mental confusion, and can produce a zombie-like, drunken state. This is a tranquilizer, so it has a downer effect. Large amounts of PCP have caused comas, convulsions, and deaths. The PCP user may feel as though his arms or legs are shrinking, may be unable to control bowel or bladder use, and may be unable to walk.

Marijuana—The physical and mental effects can last from two to four hours and include loss of coordination in various degrees, insatiable hunger, inflammation of the mucous membranes and bronchial tubes, and dilation of the pupils. The effects are similar to those caused by mild alcohol intoxication.

Often there is uncontrollable hilarity and a feeling of being beyond reality. However, large doses have been known to cause hallucination and paranoia. (Remember, grass is often cut with chemicals.) Marijuana allows the user to be more open and talkative. Marijuana intoxication is probably the most difficult drug state to detect, because an experienced user can function normally while high. Brown stains on fingertips, small burn holes in shirts or dresses, and the presence of paraphernalia (pipes, water pipes, roach chips, rolling papers, etc.) all indicate excessive use. Adults should become familiar with the marijuana symbol painted on shirts and street signs and plastered on walls. A very important sign of drug abuse is the development of tremendous apathy in the user.

Alcohol—Of course, an experienced drinker can compensate for impaired behavior due to this drug. In small doses alcohol has a tranquilizing effect; the user feels relaxed and free from tension, and inhibitions are loosened. In larger amounts, muscle coordination, memory, and judgment are affected. Alcohol may cause drowsiness in one person and act as a stimulant to another. Of course, all the usual manifestations of drunkenness are obvious: staggering, bloodshot eyes, alcohol breath, blurred vision, and often, vomiting. A hangover the next day, indicated by nausea, fatigue, severe headache, and anxiety, is a symptom of drinking abuse.

In a survey by the Johnson Institute of Minneapolis, Minnesota, 39 percent of the students questioned said they use alcohol and 21 percent said they use alcohol and other drugs. The institute also reports that the percentage of students who use alcohol at all increases markedly between the seventh and eighth grades and between the ninth and tenth grades. Moderate/heavy and heavy use increases steadily up to the eleventh grade, with the most pronounced rise in heavy use occurring between the ninth and tenth grades.[1] Are your children in these percentages?

Amphetamines—Amphetamines are stimulants that speed up the central nervous system activities. They produce a sense of well-being, alertness, and boundless energy for a short time. Pupils become dilated, appetite diminishes, and the blood pressure and respiration rate increase. While under the influence of an average dose, the user becomes overactive, irritable, suspicious to the point of paranoia, and sometimes violent. As the effect begins to diminish, the user experiences headaches, nausea, nervousness, restlessness, cotton mouth, heavy perspiration, confusion, blurred vision, and shaky hands. After the high is over, the body pace slows dramatically from its tempestuous race, causing extreme fatigue.

After months of pill use, the amphetamine user usually begins to inject (shoot up) the speed. This needle abuse brings on loss of balance, psychological dependence, noticeable weight loss, and personality changes. After a few days on the run, or cycle, the user begins to exhibit repetitive, meaningless gestures—itching, blinking, and jerky motions. At the end of the run, he must crash. If a child or a friend sleeps for several days after a week of weird behavior accompanied by tremendous weakness and depression, the odds are he is using speed. Of course, the appetite comes roaring back after the crash, which causes severe stomach cramps and muscle pains.

Many who abuse amphetamines neglect their bodies in various ways, suffering drastic weight loss, malnutrition, vitamin deficiency, and dental decay. The days without sleep cause vital organs, especially the kidneys, to suffer. Whenver a needle is involved, there is always the chance of infection and hepatitis.

Cocaine—The typical cocaine user who calls 800-COCAINE has many cocaine-related health problems. Loss of energy, insomnia, sore throat and nosebleeds, headaches, sinus problems and a runny nose are a few. Trembling, seizures or convulsions, nausea or vomiting, constant licking of lips or grinding of teeth are others. One of the early symptoms is a constant sniffing or rubbing of the nose. In regular users, loss of consciousness, trouble with breathing or swallowing, heart palpitations and lack of interest in personal health and hygiene may occur.

From a psychiatric perspective, anxiety and irritability, depression, panic, delusions and paranoia, lack of concentration, hearing voices, loss of interest in friends and non-drug related activities, memory problems, thoughts of suicide, blackouts and compulsive behavior are key indicators of cocaine dependence.

Barbiturates and Tranquilizers—These are sedatives, which means they slow down the central nervous system activities such as breathing and coordination. These drugs are readily absorbed into the bloodstream, and the effects can occur within twenty minutes. Small doses of barbiturates produce effects similar to alcohol's. Users become relaxed, drowsy, and have a false sense of well-being. The reason these drugs are so popular to slip to dates is because they cause the girls to become more jovial and social, and as a result they may lower their inhibition and impair moral judgments. Teens on barbiturates may more readily follow others' suggestions. Often, even small doses can induce sleep, but if the user remains awake he appears drunk because of his slurred speech, awkward movement and coordination, and impaired perception. Under a heavy dose, the user can lapse into a coma and even die.

Many teens don't realize they are hooked on barbiturates until they quit taking the pills. If the intake has been over a prolonged period of time, withdrawal can be as severe as *delirium tremens* or withdrawal from heroin. Usually, within five to seven hours after the regular user's last dose he begins to feel weak, dizzy, nauseated, and begins to have stomach cramps with vomiting. Heavy users have reported hallucinations during withdrawal. Breaking a sedative habit should be done with the aid of a physician.

Opiates, Heroin—Reread the section on the life of a heroin junkie, then recall that after experiencing the "rush," the user will have a feeling of detachment. A junkie can usually be detected by the dilation of his pupils and his tendency to nod off and on; his lethargy and apathy give him away.

If the user is a novice or one who uses heroin only intermittently, withdrawal will resemble the flu, causing watery eyes, runny nose, sweating, and diarrhea. If the user is a full-scale addict, withdrawal is very severe, as you may have seen on a TV show. The sickness begins four to six hours after the last injection, but becomes total hell with twelve to sixteen hours. Shakes, cramps, hot flashes, cold chills, yawning, severe aches and jerks in the back and leg muscles, vomiting, and a desperate feeling of being near death all occur. It is from here to the seventy-two-hour point (three days) that a junkie will do almost anything for a fix. The symptoms gradually diminish over the next five to ten days.

The presence of an outfit (drug injection kit) or of a cap or bag of white powder are evidence of heroin use, of course. Other telltale signs are neglected health, blood poisoning, hepatitis, tetanus, skin infection, track marks (scarred veins), ulcers, and abcesses (collections of pus in body tissue). The heroin problem is reaching epidemic proportions; the NFDA reports 400,000 daily heroin users and between two to four million occasional users.

Solvents—These are the most difficult drug habits to detect because the effects only last from five minutes to one hour. Sometimes chronic users have ulcers around the mouth and nose that will not heal. They often experience a marked weight loss. Sniffing solvents produces a zombie-like effect. Be suspicious of partly used glue or paint containers unless your child is putting them to a legitimate use, such as model-building.

In summary, there is a deterioration of moral, social, familial, and religious values, as well as a neglect of personal hygiene and appearance when drug abuse is concerned. A user is characterized by a restless, bored attitude which is exhibited not only in the dress but in the language and in the choice of friends. The individual shows a change in personality and in school-related areas such as grades, sports involvement, and attendance. There are emotional flare-ups, outbreaks of temper, and withdrawal from the family. The young drug abuser may need more money, and money may disappear. *Change is the major symptom of all drug abuse.*

The following checklist, developed by Dennis D. Nelson for use with groups of high school students, can be helpful to anyone who wants to know more about the symptoms of drug abuse.

1

Experimental Use

Junior-high-age students, especially boys, are great experimenters with various types of mood-altering substances. Some may never go beyond the experimental stage. They may decide that chemical use is not for them. But a majority of them will continue to experiment and become regular users. They will use beer and pot in this stage and will learn to seek and enjoy the mood swings that these substances will provide. A child who exhibits abuse at this stage may be establishing a lifelong pattern. Or the chemical use may level off and stay at the "social-recreational" level, causing no intrapersonal conflict or externally harmful consequences. It is difficult to assess chemical dependency at this stage. The normal turmoil of adolescence is baffling to both teenagers and their parents, and caution is advised in any evaluation procedure. Many students have been inappropriately labeled as dependent when in fact they are not. They may be using drugs, but that fact alone does not make them dependent.

2
More Regular Use

Simply using more does not, by itself, indicate dependency. But a pattern of regular use, coupled with some adverse behavioral changes, can show a definite move towards possible dependency. The point here is not how much is being used, or how often, but why it is being used and what behavioral changes occur as a result of the use. If teen-agers have to lie to their parents about their savings accounts, about why they have dropped out of school sports or other activities, or about who their companions are, and have to maintain these fictions in order to continue using drugs, they will begin to experience real guilt. Unfortunately, this guilt produces feelings of intense self-hate, which results in increased drug use. A cycle of use-guilt-remorse-increased-use begins.

3
Daily Preoccupation

Preoccupation with drugs is one of the major indicators of a chemical problem. More and more of the student's time, energy and money are spent on thinking about being high and insuring that a steady supply of drugs is available. Questioning a user at this stage will reveal that very few of his or her daily activities do not include drug use. The user accepts this as normal. Problems with parents or police may serve to cause the abuser to decide that it would be smart to cut down or to quit using all together. And they may succeed for a few weeks. Generally, though, these periods of abstinence will not last. They do

112

serve, however, to strengthen the abuser's sincere delusion that because he or she "quit," there is no problem. It can be pointed out to the abuser that, even though he or she feels that there is still a choice as to whether or not to use, the "choice" is always the same: to keep using.

4
Dependency

By the time the user has reached a state of dependency, negative personal feelings have been building steadily until they require daily, even hourly, medication with drugs. Abusers in this state are unable to distinguish between normal and intoxicated behavior. To them, being high is normal, and no rationale or moral argument can break through their chemically maintained delusion. This delusion persists even in the face of overwhelming evidence that his or her abuse is out of control and is physically, mentally, and emotionally strangling him or her. The abuser will continue to insist that there is no problem, that it is not out of control, and that he or she can quit at any time.[2]

(From the Adolescent Chemical Use Chart © Dennis D. Nelson. Published by CompCare Publications, Minneapolis, Minnesota 55441. Reprinted by permission.)

What Do You Think?

1. What are the most obvious changes you first note in a person who has begun using drugs? Can you usually spot a drug user?
2. If you know someone who has begun using drugs,

should you attempt to help? If it is a friend, should you immediately abandon that friendship? How can you continue in the friendship without you yourself becoming tempted to use drugs?

3. Why is it important to select your friends wisely? What are some of the qualities you should look for in establishing a friendship?

4. Which is more important—a person's attitudes or his actions? How does one affect the other?

5. Not everyone can be a leader. What is wrong with following the crowd?

8.

The Response of the Home: Prevention at the Grass Roots

IN DESCRIBING A SOLUTION TO THE drug dilemma, the message of John the Baptist is appropriate: "And now also the axe is laid unto the root of the trees..." (Matt. 3:10). This "grass-roots" prevention must take place where drug abuse and alcoholism most often begin—in the home.

Definition of a Home

One dictionary defines a home as "a congenial abiding place where loved ones share life; a place of affection, peace and rest; a unit of society." It has already been stated that the average home is failing to live up to its definition; as a result, America as a whole and our children in particular are the losers. Never before in the history of our nation has there been such an attack on the home. It seems as if Satan himself has declared war. It is not enough to recognize the symptoms; we must probe deeper to find the causes. A basic tenet of behavioral psychology is that all behavior is caused, and it is unanimous that the number one cause of deviant behavior is the breakdown of the home. A fractured family fails to provide children with an opportunity to develop healthy attitudes and self-images. Increasing numbers of parents each year are reaching the ends of their ropes. What can we do about the problems our children are having? It is obvious that many desperately need wisdom and guidance.

As a parent, I am grateful that there is a Book of wisdom and guidance to help give direction to my children so they will not choose to experiment with drugs. This book is found in the wisdom literature of the Bible. The Book of Proverbs, written about twenty-seven hundred years ago, offers examples from nature that help us and give us the means and counsel to protect our children from yielding to temptation. The Septuagint (the ancient Greek version) and the Vulgate (the ancient Latin version) translated Proverbs 30:24 as "These are wiser than wise." Agur writes:

(v. 24) There are four things which are little on the earth but they are exceedingly wise; (v. 25) The ants are a people not strong yet they prepare their meat in the summer; (v. 26) The conies are but a feeble folk, yet they make their houses in the rocks; (v. 27) The locusts have no king, yet they go forth all of them by bands; (v. 28) The spider taketh hold with her hands, and is in Kings' palaces.

THE ANTS—Preparation

Ants prepare their food in the summer while there is still time before the winter's cold and snow. The word "prepare" comes from the Latin word *paro*, meaning "to make ready," "to equip," "to make complete." There are a number of things prepared parents can do to prevent the spread of drug abuse. If your children are pre-teens or if drugs have not reached your home yet, then it is still "summertime," so you had better begin preparing for the winter storms soon will be raging. There is a nationwide drug epidemic, and there is no home beyond or above the possiblity of a drug problem.

First, you can be a good example in word, conduct, and attitude. Children deserve and must have a living example.

If you want your children to handle their emotions, then don't overreact and fly off the handle about every little thing. Well-behaved children are imitating well-behaved parents. If you desire your children to have clean mouths, then you must keep yours clean of all profanity.

Parents, Don't Disqualify Yourselves

Parents, learn how to enjoy life. If you don't, then don't expect your children to. Set a good example by respecting drugs yourselves. You can expect your children to model their drug-taking attitudes after yours. The Johnson Institute feels its studies show a strong correlation between use and misuse rates in adolescents and the standards of their parents.[1]

I regret that so many "experts" suggest you drink in moderation. My research and my own experience proves that parents who abuse their bodies and minds with drugs—alcohol, tobacco, pills—disqualify themselves from the task of counseling their children. This book portrays drug abuse as a roaring lion and alcohol as a poisonous serpent. I seriously doubt that any parent would ever allow either of these dangers into the home.

It is wise to remember that the family medicine chest is often the source of a child's initial drug experience. Most medicine chests are stockpiles of drugs no longer needed; easy access to diet pills, tranquilizers, sleeping pills, and pain pills is a key factor to the "great turn-on." The drinking parent who forbids his child to take drugs is a hypocrite in his child's eyes. The drug lecture I got on the evils of marijuana was not very effective when delivered by my drunken stepfather.

The argument of moderation obviously fails to define what moderation is, because millions are crossing that fine line to problem drinking. The drink taken to relax after a long day teaches children that the stresses of the daily routine of life require chemical and artificial relief. It also displays a bored and restless attitude and sets an example of escapism.

In surveys among youth, 65 percent of students polled said, "Yes, my parents use drugs."[2] The surveys didn't distinguish between legal or illegal drug use, and neither did the kids. They just recognized the fact that their parents were drug users. This is an automatic recommendation of drug use to a child. You may say, "Oh, I need this to relax, to sleep, to help me with my nerves," but your children don't recognize the pharmacy labels, only the fact that, "Yes, my parents use drugs."

Total Prevention

Prevention means preparation now, and preparation means parents equipping themselves for the task and privilege of raising a child to be best equipped for life. You are not a parent simply because you had a baby—almost anyone can have children. You are a parent only when you provide for and prepare that child to be ready for life.

As parents, we are concerned with physical development. This includes seeing that our children are properly fed, involved in adequate exercise, given physical checkups and vitamin supplements, and otherwise cared for.

We are to be concerned with their mental development. We should want our children to attend the best possible schools and should encourage cultural interest such as music, drama, art and literature. It is imperative for parents to encourage good reading habits by having the right kind of reading materials around the house. The influence that filthy magazines have on impressionable young people is tragic. It used to be difficult to find these kinds of publications, but now many youth see them in their own homes.

Many children must be motivated to get excited about learning. Encourage your child to ask questions. Learn together about the stars, oceans, animals, sports, and history. Teach them the why and how of living. A great truth for parents to remember is—"You will be the same in the next five years as you are today, except for the people you meet, the places you travel, the books you read."

Of course, I believe the Bible is the greatest Book ever written. The Bible is a sociology Book that teaches how to relate to and live with others and a psychology Book that helps us to understand ourselves and find peace with ourselves. It is a road map for the future and a love letter to us from God. Encouraging children to properly prepare and equip themselves includes Bible reading.

Much has been written on the role music plays in the area of mental development. While your children are still young, break the habit of listening just to body music, because it can prevent you (and them) from enjoying *heart* and *head* music. You need to check out the type of music your children are listening to by listening to it yourself, by reading the album cover, front and back. In our home we like to begin the day with inspirational gospel music. Then, during the afternoon and evening, we often listen to classical and contemporary albums. I enjoy music that moves me on the inside rather than that which only moves me on the outside.

Cultural interests and talents are lying dormant in most children. As parents, we need to encourage our children to excel in at least one cultural area. Children are very talented and imaginative and should be given the opportunity to express themselves and develop their God-given talents. In short, let us turn our homes into the incubators promoting growth, rather than trash cans containing the world's smut.

Parents can prepare themselves by keeping in touch with the world around them and with the world of their children. Most young people view their parents as old-fashioned and "out of it" because the parents don't know what is happening in life. There are scores of helpful books available, and it is tragic that television documentaries, magazines, and newspaper articles on drug abuse or moral problems are ignored by most parents. Many teens are screaming on the inside, "Help me, Daddy. Help me, Mother. Help me to understand drugs. Help me to understand sex. Help me to understand me."

THE LOCUSTS—Unity

"The locusts have no king [leader] yet they go forth all of them by bands" (Prov. 30:27). This unity is the locusts' only source of strength. Alone, each is insignificant, but united, they are mighty and destructive swarms. Unity is the key to a harmonious home. It would be wise to remember the words of

Jesus, later quoted by Abraham Lincoln: "Every city or house divided against itself shall not stand" (Matt. 12:25). A house without unity will never be a home. Since the definition of the word "unity" is "oneness" (from the Latin word *uniat*), our reference to unity is that loving oneness that meets the most basic needs of man: the need to belong and the need for security.

Most homes take on one of two appearances. One is the appearance of prison, in which everyone lives in his own little cell or microcosm (his own world), having little or no communication with others. It is ironic that we have the ability to communicate with astronauts in space, when parents often are unable to communicate with each other or with their children. As I travel across the nation, I hear the same cries. "My husband doesn't give me the time of day." Or, "My parents never have time to listen." In this day of amazing communication, many families don't really communicate and relate to each other.

The other appearance given by many homes is that of a battlefield, where members of the family are constantly wounding each other. Civil war is raging in many homes. One of the horrors of the War Between the States was that it pitted brother against brother and even father against son. We need another surrender at the Appomattox Court House, so to speak.

Unity in the home attracts like a magnet. Just as the light from a candle draws the moth, the light and warmth from two parents in love and united in life draws the children to their parents. Lack of this unity drives children away, depriving them of security and instilling in them a sense of inadequacy. As a result, children develop a loser's philosophy that causes them to have poor relationships with others.

They do not learn how to give and take. Instead they learn: "It's either my way, or no way at all."

The vast majority of troubled teens I counsel cannot remember their families ever doing much together. Members of a fractured and fragmented family often feel they have nothing in common. In an effort to spend time with my child, I give my little girl at least one hour a day of my undivided attention. It is her hour; we do whatever she wants to do. Most homes need to call a ceasefire, or truce, on backbiting, clawing, and chewing on one another with cruel remarks. Lack of unity wounds the spirit, and a wounded spirit causes rebellion.

The family needs to be united in *direction, duty, discipline,* and *dedication.* Parents can overcome division by calling a family conference to determine goals for every member of the family.

United in Directions

Unity of direction will prevent children from playing divide-and-conquer with parents by pitting one against the other. It doesn't accomplish much for mother to encourage the child to practice the piano if dad insists music is sissy and complains about the racket. I know a couple who are divided on the educational goal for their child. The mother wants her son to read many of the outstanding books available, but the father considers such reading silly and a waste of time.

A mother's concern about a child's spiritual growth can be stifled if dad refuses to attend church, refuses to read the Bible, or if he otherwise provides a poor example. I have seen teens greatly confused by parents who cannot agree. There is a need for a clear and well-defined direction that the family will travel together.

United in Duty

The family also must share duties around the house. Most husbands have no idea how much work the average wife does in one day. There must be an even delegation of the chores. For years, mothers have had to face diapers, dishes, and cleaning alone, while preschool children constantly demand their full attention. My college psychology professor taught that men and women can tolerate stress and pressure much better if they know someone else realizes what they are enduring. Not only should the father be grateful for a job well done, he should be helpful.

United in Discipline

The family also should be united in discipline. The Bible teaches that children are to be disciplined, because there is no way a child can teach himself to be good. However, no one has to teach a child to disobey, to rebel, or to be just plain bad. As a Christian parent, I desire my children to revere God and to respect authority. The reason teens seem to have little respect for parents, school, church, and the law is because they have no respect for authority— period. There are certain words many "child experts" are trying to remove from our vocabulary; one is the word "discipline" and another is "chastise." This has resulted in an epidemic of permissiveness that is on the verge of being a national disaster.

Many teachers refer to schools as "battle zones" or "blackboard jungles." Teachers and their personal effects are fair game in some school systems; attack on teachers by students, and damaging of personal property are not that uncommon. Many teachers are suffering from stress, the stress of disciplining vicious kids. A teacher in Portsmouth, Virginia, said, "I have been teaching for twenty-one years, and I have seen changes. Today, students are *self*-centered and have no respect for the teacher, property, or any authority. There is no learning when you spend all your time on discipline."

The word "discipline" comes from the same Greek word that translates "disciple," meaning "to be a learner." When I discipline my child with love and consistency, I am helping her learn self-control, responsibility, and respect for authority. A rebellious and disobedient three-year-old grows up into a rebellious and disobedient teen-ager. Discipline should begin at an early age. The parent should always make clear before, during, and after each discipline session how much he loves the child. A young couple I know teaches their children, "I love you too much to let you act like this." Explain to the child that all of us are held accountable by God and by society for our actions.

Self-discipline (on the endangered species list in America) is the natural result of external discipline. As a child learns discipline, he learns to say no to various temptations. Children who are disciplined in love develop a strong desire to please their parents; as they learn about the love of God, they will desire to please their heavenly Father. I desire the very best for my children, and I want them to achieve great things. But if I don't teach them how to control themselves, I have failed. Proverbs teaches, "He that is slow to anger is better than the mighty; and he that ruleth his spirit than he that taketh a city" (Prov. 16:32). The one who can control, restrain, and discipline himself will be a champion.

The word "chasten" means "to make chaste, to make pure, to make holy." Proverbs again offers instruction when it states, "Chasten thy son while there is hope..." (Prov. 19:18). As I travel across our nation, I can easily discern those who have been disciplined at home and those who have not. The father should be like a shepherd whose "rod and staff" comfort his sheep. The rod is used for correction and discipline and the staff for protection. If both parents accept the Bible as the authority for the home, they will be united in disciplinary strategy.

Parents should take the time and effort to find out in which areas they will enforce discipline. I know many couples who are divided in the essential area of correction. The mother may try to help her child learn respect for others, respect for authority, and self-discipline, but the father may be lazy or apathetic and is therefore lenient. This is like splitting a child in half by pulling his arms in opposite directions.

I have often encountered the mentality that believes, "I love my child too much to spank or hurt him." What a foolish statement! Consider these words from the Book of Proverbs: "He that spareth his rod hateth his son: but he that loveth him chasteneth him betimes" (Prov. 13:24). "The rod and reproof give wisdom: but a child left to himself bringeth his mother to shame" (Prov. 29:15). When a child learns that rebellion, disobedience, self-indulgence, and sin bring pain and displeasure, he has learned wisdom. No wonder there are thousands of parents alone, forsaken, and forgotten in rest homes—they never taught their children responsibility.

The Book of Proverbs offers this promise from God: "Train up a child in the way he should go: and when he is old, he will not depart from it" (Prov. 22:6). The word "train" means "to mold character; to instruct by example and exercise; to drill; to make obedient to orders; to point in an exact direction; to prepare for contest or battle." Discipline is not punishment for stepping out of line, but rather instruction for the child on the way he should go and grow.

"A good home is authoritarian, for if a wise mother sees her young son about to eat poison berries, she stops him. She does not say: 'I must not coerce him. He must make his own discovery of truth....' but a good home is also an honoring of the personality. So any sound education is both authoritarian and free."[3]

United in Dedication

Members of the family must be united in their dedication to each other. Dr. Kenneth Kenniston, author of *The Uncommitted*, calls this "the age of the uncommitted." One reason a teen-ager is so committed to the gang or to the peer group is because he has never experienced commitment to the family. Parents should let their children know of their dedication to each other. My children should know there will never be a day when I will go off and leave them or their mother. Little good to hear daddy say, "I would protect you even if it meant death for me," if daily they see daddy refusing to *live* for them. Spouses should be dedicated to each other. Use your energies to make your marriage and your family a success.

Because the nuclear family is so small (two parents and children), the margin for error is small. In times past, families were much larger and closer together. If there was a drunken father, a troubled mother, or if one parent was brutal, at least a grandparent, an uncle or aunt, or an older brother was available to help overcome that detrimental influence. But today the extended family is usually separated by hundreds of miles. Many families have no time for church, where children might otherwise have contact with supportive and sympathetic adults.

A college professor once told our class, "One bad parent is a dangerous dilemma, but two bad parents form a disaster." Today the problem is compounded by the rise in the divorce rate; there are twelve to fifteen million children in one-parent homes, with the majority being reared by the mother. Absence of the father is considered the strongest factor in juvenile delinquency. This absence is not always due to desertion or divorce; it often occurs because of a job in which the father travels constantly so that he can have a higher income.

The trend of the 1980s is this: one out of every two marriages ends in divorce. Half of our children will be living in a broken home before they reach the age of eighteen.

A man and a woman dedicated to each other can make a marriage work. My child should know I am dedicated to his mother by my actions, and I expect my wife to be dedicated to the family. Togetherness is the key. My wife and I have adopted the slogan of a church building program as our family philosophy: "Together we build." "Play together, work together, and pray together" should become the family golden rule.

In this age of materialism it is wise to remember that your children would rather have you than all the trinkets overtime money can buy. I met a young couple so dedicated to their family that the father turned down a promotion just so he could have his evenings and weekends with his children. Unity will turn your house into a home.

WHY DO I NEED A HOME?

Someone asked the question: "What is a home? A roof to keep out the rain? Four walls to keep out the wind? Floors to protect from the cold?" Yes, a house provides all those protections, but a home is much more. It has been wisely said that a home is the cry of a baby; the song of a mother; the strength of a father; the warmth of loving hearts; the light of happy eyes; kindness, loyalty, and comradeship.

The home is the first church and school for your young ones, where they learn what is right and wrong and what is good and kind; where they go for comfort when they are hurt or sick; where joy is shared and sorrow is eased; where fathers and mothers are respected and loved; where children are wanted. That's a home. Billy Graham calls the home a place "where even the teakettle sings out for happiness."

An anonymous writer asks: "Why do I need a home? I was born in a hospital, educated in schools and college, courted in an automobile, married in a church. I live out of a delicatessen—tin cans and paper bags. I spend my morning on the golf course, afternoons at bridge parties, my evenings at the movies. And when I die I will be cremated and buried in a brass urn. All I really need is a garage." What a terrible cynicism about such a wonderful place. Unfortunately, many share these feelings.

"This is the true nature of home—it is a place of peace; the shelter, not only from all injury, but from all terror, doubt, and division."[4]

THE ROCK BADGER—Building on the Rock

Another of the four animals that provide models for human wisdom is the cony, or the rock badger. "The badgers are but a feeble folk, yet they make their houses in the rocks" (Prov. 30:26). This small animal realizes its own limitations and weaknesses. Out of desire to provide for and protect its family, the badger builds his home in the safety of the rocks. The rocks afford protection from the plains fires and from the waters of flood. When other animals are destroyed or left homeless, the badger is high and safe in the rocks. Thus the badger is a model for the use of skills and resourcefulness to gain protection from the elements and adversaries.

Another badger trait that can instruct us is his habit of posting sentries on the lookout to warn, help, and protect. Consequently, badgers are hard to capture, and it is no wonder they are called wiser than wise. A home built in the safety of the rocks is the sure foundation upon which preparation, unity, and the ability to take advantage of every opportunity can be built. No matter how much energy and planning, work and money you put into your house, if you don't build it on a solid foundation you can lose it all. Remember, no house is stronger than its foundation.

An itinerant preacher named Jesus pointed out the necessity of building on a proper foundation in His Sermon on the Mount.

Therefore, whosoever heareth these sayings of mine, and doeth them, I will liken him unto a wise man, which built his house upon a rock: And the rain descended, and the floods came, and the winds blew, and beat upon that house; and *it fell not:* for it was founded upon a rock. And every one that heareth these sayings of mine, and doeth them not, shall be likened unto a foolish man, which built his house upon the sand: And the rain descended, and the floods came, and the winds blew, and beat upon that house; and *it fell:* and great was the fall of it (Matt. 7:24–27, italics mine).

Notice, if you will, that both builders tried to make their houses attractive and sturdy, and both used fine materials, but one took a shortcut, possibly out of laziness or ignorance, and didn't dig deeply enough to build his house on a solid rock foundation. Notice also that the same storm hit each home, but the one without the rock foundation fell, and terrible was the fall. You can have costly furniture with beautifully coordinated wallpaper, fine draperies, exquisite antiques, plush carpet, and you can do your best as a parent, be successful in business, and be an active supporter of your community, but the storm clouds will come and the rains will fall. Will your house stand?

History tells of mankind's many uses for rocks through the ages. Rocks have been used for foundations, dwelling places, altars, and for refreshing shade. In the Bible, the rock is a symbol of Christ Himself. The Word of God plainly teaches that it is only in a personal relationship with the living Christ that we can find stability, security, and strength. I have done what millions of others have done: I have built my life, my family, and my future on the Rock of Christ Himself. Consider these verses in your Bible: Deuteronomy 32:4, 32:31; Psalms 9:9, 27:5, 31:3,

40:2; Psalm 46 (this has been called the Song of the House on the Rock). Paul refers to Christ as being the Rock in 1 Corinthians 10:4.

THE SPIDER—Opportunity

The fourth example of wisdom offered by the animal kingdom is that of the spider. "The spider taketh hold with her hands, and is in the kings' palaces" (Prov. 30:28). The spider has several enviable characteristics that every parent should possess. It has the virtues of ingenuity, patience, persistence, and, most of all, it has the ability to take advantage of every opportunity. The only explanation for finding spiders in both cottages of the poor and the palaces of kings is their ability to find and take advantage of openings. A door left ajar, a window left open, a crack in the wall—they all provide opportunities for the spider to set up housekeeping. After preparation and unity comes the ability to take advantage of every opportunity.

Most parents fail to realize the tremendous opportunities they have when their children are young. In the early stages of a child's life, parents are able to build bridges between themselves and their child that will allow passage in the years to come. Yet most parents fail to realize this great opportunity. This bridge of communication is the greatest asset a child can have in the perilous teen-age years to come.

Quality Communication Is a Must

There seems to be a great deal of interest in the area of communication, yet much of the information available is too technical. The word needs to be defined in a language people can understand. One dictionary defines "communicate" as "to share in; to have in common; to cause others to partake in; the ability to talk freely."

It is interesting to note that the word translated "communicate" is the Greek word for *koinonia*, which is also translated "fellowship." *Koinonia* means to have in common, to share with freely, to partake in. The original meaning relates to sharing with others in order to meet their needs; the word is also translated "communion," "companion," and "partner." In Christian circles the word *koinonia* is popular because of the interest in small sharing and fellowship groups.

I believe the Lord intended for the home to be a small sharing group and a place of fellowship. Fellowship means two fellows in the same ship, both paddling toward the same port. It is so important for the family to be united in direction. A lack of fellowship, or communication, is one reason why so many ships are sinking, and why teen-agers are abandoning the sinking ships.

Parents, don't forfeit the great opportunity to communicate when your children are young, because the older they get, the more difficult it is to influence them. They become wise with worldly wisdom and less receptive to your ideas. Besides, if you wait too long to put in the lines of communications, they won't be sturdy enough to withstand the storms of adolescence. Statistics show it is urgent to reach your children at an early age.

Earlier in the book, I quoted the Johnson Institute's report on the marked increase in drug use between the seventh and eighth grades. Its conclusion is that prevention needs to begin by seventh grade, since by the eighth grade more than one-half of the students use alcohol and one in ten uses substantial amounts regularly.

Without question, there is a discrepancy between what parents believe about drug use and what is actually happening in schools. Parents need to take their blinders off and see the awful truth.

Your children will only be young once, and if they don't receive the help only you can give, they will be searching for the rest of their lives. Parents need to establish communication now, since without it problems wil become worse and worse. Problems don't solve themselves; they only become more serious. Many parents ignore a problem because they believe time will solve it or the child or teen will outgrow it.

The adage "Time heals all wounds" can be dangerously inaccurate. If a wound is infected, time will only make it worse. Eventually it may result in the loss of a limb. In the same way, time will not heal bitterness, resentment, or rebellion. In fact, time will only make these worse.

I believe this is one reason we have so much abnormal rebellion. A basic psychological tenet is that normal rebellion leads to maturity and opens up communication. It is through conflict that family members learn to solve problems, learn to respect the rights of others, and learn to understand each other. Normal rebellion leads the teen to try his own wings to see if he can make it on his own; it encourages him to leave the nest when he is completely prepared to leave. Abnormal rebellion, the result of careless indifference, is destructive. It shuts the door of communication and isolates family members from one another.

Parents need to remember the universal law of the

Bible: You will reap what you sow (see Gal. 6:7). Teen-agers who have been wounded in spirit will get even. They can flunk school, steal a car, get busted, run away, get married too young, or proudly announce, "I'm pregnant." Many young offenders have confessed to me, "I did it to get even for all the times they never had time for me."

Fellowship means to have things in common, and sharing life requires *time, tone,* and a *testimony*—a life that qualifies you to help your children. To keep the lines of communication open you must have time for your children and let them know it. Love could be spelled t-i-m-e. Never be too busy to listen to their problems. If you don't have time to listen to how he got a hit at the ballgame or to see the picture she drew at school, then don't expect them to bother you with dating, sex, or drug problems. Time is a must for an open and loving relationship.

Israel's King David was too busy building armies and kingdoms to build his family. Be accessible! Jesus, with His busy schedule, had time for people with problems, including little children. He was approachable. Fellowship and communication involve partnership. I want to be a partner in my child's life. This means I will make the time to enjoy her activities, and I will take inventory of my family's activities. I recently saw a car with two bumper stickers: "The family that prays together stays together" and "The family that plays together stays together." I believe both are true.

In all of my research on building family unity, I have observed a common thread holding many homes together—outdoor activities (camping, hiking, picnics, and playing at the park) seem to be invaluable. There is great value in being away from the phone,

the stores, the television, and just being together—
seeing God's beautiful handiwork by day and sitting by an open fire laughing, talking, and sharing
by night.

Many anthropologists and paleontologists consider fire one of mankind's greatest discoveries for two
reasons. The first is obvious: fire cooks food and
provides warmth and protection. Curt P. Richester, a
Johns Hopkins behavioral scientist, offers another
fascinating reason: "The fire made it possible for all
members of the family, young and old, to sit around
and face each other, look into the fire and think.
This situation offered opportunities for strong attachments between members of the family to develop."[5]

No doubt families have enjoyed the tranquility of
the fire as they have dreamt about the future and
shared ideas and fears and goals. I may not be able
to afford a plush motor home or a fine lodge, but I
can afford a pup tent. It is in this time with my
children that I hope to meet some of their greatest
needs.

One of those needs is to learn how to handle
stress and pressure. Years ago, when the majority of
families either lived in rural settings or worked together
in factories, the children watched mom and dad
almost twenty-four hours a day. They saw dad work
to save the crops, or work until his hands were
bleeding. The children saw their parents handle
stress. But today most children have never seen
parents at their place of employment. I advise every
parent to make arrangements for the children to see
dad and mom under work pressure.

Another basic childhood need psychologists remind us of is the need for adventure. Adventure, of
course, means a thrill, a stirring experience, a risky

or exciting event. It would be wise for us to remember that those who are the most attracted to drugs are those who are bored or discontented with life. Life should be exciting and fulfilling. Helen Keller was blind and deaf from infancy but became a great writer and lecturer. She said, "Life is a daring adventure, or nothing at all."

By example, parents show life as a matter of existing or enduring or of living vibrantly, constantly learning and loving. Many parents show by the emptiness in their lives that life for them is like an incurable disease. Someone said, "Life protracted is protracted woe." Life is one long process of getting tired, according to many parents' attitudes. Of course, you can, by your life, show your children that life is exciting, exhilarating, and worth living.

One reason man, regardless of age, escapes through chemical means is that he is just plain bored. This is sometimes called the "pleasure syndrome." If you desire to take advantage of the opportunities to prevent your children from being devoured by the roaring lion of drug abuse, one of the things you can do is to encourage your child at an appropriate age to join you in an exciting hobby.

Every parent should sit down with his children who are in or near the drug-abuse age for an "I care" session. Start with, "Son, it is natural to want adventure, but don't miss the boat and drown. Don't look for thrills and adventure in the wrong place." Aesop's fable, *The Dog and the Shadow,* warns, "Beware lest you lose substance by grasping at the shadow." This is good advice for young people today.

A wise parent suggests, "Let's explore together." One of the contributing factors in the drug problem is teen-age boredom. The cry that "there is nothing to do" should be translated: "There is nothing meaningful to do." Years ago, teens had to work, or the family would have perished. But today, the only thing many teens need to do is stay out of trouble and not cause embarrassment. To an ever-increasing number of teens, it seems the only dangerous and exciting activity is in the drug scene.

One of the cardinal sins a parent can commit is to be overprotective. I counseled a young man who had just been busted, and we talked about the restlessness of teens and the need for adventure and excitement. He told me of his domineering mother, who smothered him with baby treatment. All his life she had forbidden him to ride a horse, to play football, to go water or snow skiing, or to go camping because these activities were too dangerous. So he sought an artificial thrill in the drug scene, and it almost cost him his life.

Personally, I would rather my son or daughter run the risk of breaking a leg playing football or skiing than ruin his or her mind and body in the drug scene. I now realize that scuba diving, learning to fly a plane, karate, sports, learning to play an instrument, traveling, or just plain learning, all provide far greater thrills for teens and their parents than do artificial, destructive chemicals. All these activities develop sound bodies and sound minds and teach responsibility. Parents, *don't prohibit without providing adequate substitutes*. After my "born-again" experience I didn't just quit the drug scene; I filled that gap with positive alternatives. Now that cheap and plastic scene has no attraction for me.

Yes, there are many problems in life, but children can see you handle the pressure, examine the possibilities, and solve the problems instead of being crushed by their weight or running away from them. The most convincing statement you make is your way of living. Soon your children will compare you to Johnny's parents, who are always fighting, yelling, smoking, or drinking. Imagine the opportunity you will have when they ask why don't you smoke, yell, or drink. You will have a chance to share the importance of a full and meaningful life. You can explain, "We love you so much that mom and dad have found a way to cope with life that will help us to live longer and that will prove to you that drinking, smoking, and drugs are less than the best."

Parents should wear the same shoes they want their children to fill. It takes time to be a companion, to share life together, to be a partner. Parents have the right and the duty to know where their children are, who they are with, where they are going. Don't be afraid to check on them. But remember, you're not a policeman—you're a parent!

A second ingredient of communication is tone. The tone of your voice and of your spirit will influence the atmosphere of your home and your child's developing self-image. As parents we have the awesome responsibility of showing our children what genuine love really is. Genuine love gives birth to courage and security. Teens crave the security of their peer group when they have no security at home. Psychologists have repeatedly told parents that the greatest security a person can have is in relationships that don't change. Being a teen-ager is rough and frustrating enough without the added problem of frustrated parents.

In many of my counseling experiences I have dealt with disturbed parents and the problems their teen-agers were experiencing. I soon realized that the parent's problem was not just in his relationship to the child, but also in his relationship to his mate. Mothers with unfulfilled needs will be overprotective, overbearing, and overwhelming. Most teen-agers' problems usually vanish when their parents work out their own problems. Most parents would never admit this, but usually they are more concerned with the trouble the teen is causing them in terms of mate relationship, aggravation, and social embarrassment than they are with the child himself.

When this is true in a home, there is little effort to really communicate and help. Instead, the mother or father will ask everyone and anyone to help straighten out their son or daughter, complaining all the while about their situation but never really stopping to work it out themselves. It has been said that teens don't cause problems; they only reveal existing problems. Your attitude toward your mate and children will largely determine whether there will be any real and positive communication in your home.

One of the greatest things I can do for my children is love their mother. If I make it a top priority to meet my wife's needs, then I have gone a long way in meeting my children's needs. Frustration, jealousy, insecurity, and anxiety are easily passed from mother to child. As fathers, we need to be like Joseph— protecting his Mary and son Jesus from the Herods of the world. Always be careful in the tone you take with your children.

Parents often take the whole day's frustrations out on the children. Parents also tend to put children in categories. Labels are very powerful, and children seldom rise above them. Karl Menninger has said, "Diagnostic name calling may be damning.... The very word 'cancer' is said to have killed some patients long before the malignancy did them in. If labels are so decisive to the physical well-being of an adult, how much more fateful must they be for the developing personality of a growing child."[6]

Parents should never ridicule their children about things that are important to the children. Don't treat older boys and girls like babies; allow them their privacy and certain freedoms. This kind of communion, or tone, in the home will encourage children to bring friends home. As a family, always have room for your children's friends. A party, a ball game, or a camping trip are all great ways to tell the gang, "I love my child, I'm a part of his life, and I also care about you."

Communication means fellowship, and fellowship means to share with, to have in common, to be able to talk freely. Invitations like, "Let's go bowling" or "Let's play a game of pinball" are welcome words to the ears of a child. Also, communication (*koinonia*) is translated "communion," which is a harmonious, mutual participation of thoughts, ideas, and feelings. Is the tone of your home like a refreshing symphony that unites, or is it like a blaring rock concert that drives the family apart? I don't want my tone to drive my children away; I want to draw them to me. If we spend the time to establish the right tone, our children will think we are the greatest because we make them feel important. It has been said that discipline has no real meaning unless it comes from two parents who have demonstrated great love for each other and for the children.

I don't want my children to learn about and make life's most important decisions with someone else. I love my child so much that the tone (atmosphere) in our home will be such to cause her to come to us with her concerns and questions about sex, career planning, the origin of life, and eternal destinies.

Prevention of problems no longer need have a negative meaning. It is, instead, a matter of taking advantage of every opportunity. "Opportunity" means a "fit time," or an especially right time or moment. It comes from the Latin word *opportunus,* which means "favorable"—literally, a favorable wind blowing toward the port. For your sake, your children's sake, and our country's sake, take advantage of every opportunity. If there is a special show on television, an interesting article in the paper, a noted speaker in town—share it together and then discuss it.

The most favorable wind is blowing now if your children are young. You must train your child while he is still a child. John Bisagno, pastor of First Baptist Church in Houston, Texas, made the statement, "I have revamped my whole schedule and philosophy. I have turned down almost all extra speaking engagements to be with my boys. Right now they want daddy, but soon they will discover girls, and they won't know if I'm there." The Bible, in Ecclesiastes 3:1,2, offers this wisdom: "To every thing there is a season, and a time to every purpose under the heaven: A time to be born, and a time to die; a time to plant, and a time to pluck up that which is planted...." Take the time to learn your child's thoughts, to discuss his goals and failures, his desires and questions.

The following questions are taken from *Questions and Answers About Drug Abuse* by Robert DuPont, M. D., of the Special Action Office for Drug Abuse Prevention and the National Institute on Drug Abuse.

Read them as a family and answer them honestly. They may open new lines of communication for you.

Drugs and Drinking

THE REACH QUIZ

1. When was the last time you and he had a serious discussion? What was it about?

2. Can you tell, without his telling you, when he's feeling angry? How? What about when he's feeling happy? Proud? Guilty? Sad? Afraid? How do you express those feelings?

3. If you could change his appearance in any way, what would you do? Cut his hair? Throw away his faded jeans? Make him stand straighter? What do you think you would change in his appearance? What do you think he would change in yours?

4. You've worked very late for about two weeks in a row. All you can think of tonight is a good, long sleep. But he reminds you it's Little League championship game. Or you get a surprise bonus vacation, but it has to be taken while he's in school. What do you do? How does your family handle a legitimate conflict of interests? Do you compromise? Does the one with the most desperate need have it his way? Does the one who gets his way promise to make up for it in the future?

5. What do you think he really wants to do when he starts a career? Do you approve? Would you approve of anything he wanted to be? A circus roustabout? A nuclear physicist? A poet? What do you think he thinks of your career?

6. Do you think he knows what your real interests are? What do you think he thinks? Do you think he approves?

7. Do you think he has any special talents? What? What do you think he feels his special talents are? What do you think he feels yours are?

8. Name two things you think make him feel most angry. Happiest. Proudest. Guiltiest. Saddest. Most afraid. What do you think he thinks provokes these feelings in you?

9. Do you think he has any major shortcomings? What? What do you think he feels yours are?

10. Do you think he likes you? Not loves, son-to-parent style, but likes? Do you think he would choose you as a friend if you weren't his parent? Would you choose him?

GOD'S PLAN FOR PARENTS

Henry Brandt, author and Christian psychologist, has often said, "Adequate parents must be adequate partners, and before a person can be an adequate partner, he must be an adequate person." Before you can have peace with others, you must have peace with yourself, and that happens only when you have peace with God. Here are several suggestions to help you like yourself, to help you be an adequate person, to help you have a real and exciting life.

Realize there is a holy, loving, all-knowing personal Creator who has a blueprint for your life. Notice that an attribute of the heavenly Father is holiness. In this day and age of overemphasis on the love of God and underemphasis on His holiness, we must be reminded that He is holy and man is not. The reason our past is soiled, our present is snarled, and our future is uncertain is that we have sinned against and rebelled against the holy God. "All we like sheep have gone astray; we have turned every one to his own way..." (Isa. 53:6). Our sin is made manifest by our active rebellion or passive indifference.

The second attribute of the heavenly Father is His love. Law and love have no quarrel. The greatest news I ever heard was the fact that God loved me, even though I was a rebel and had violated His law. This love of God is something that needs to be experienced and believed. It is the ultimate proof that God loves you in the person of Jesus Christ. Jesus knows what it is to be lonely, afraid, betrayed, tired, and in great pain. Jesus also knows what it is like to lose a loved one. But the greatest demonstration of His love for us is His death on a cross. The Cross proves we are sinners and in need of the Savior, but it also proves the love of God, in that He agonized and died to save us from our sins and set us free. Love is a synonym for God. Ask the Lord to reveal His love to you.

The third attribute of God is His omniscience. Omniscient means "all knowing." God is the "all-knowing God"—He knows everything. Acts 15:18 tells us, "Known unto God are all his works from the beginning of the world." This covers past, present, and future. Our lives are an open book to Him. We can't hide from God; we must take personal responsibility for our problems. Jesus said, "out of the heart" of man comes every problem (Matt. 15:19). Usually we are our own worst enemies. Most of us like to blame others (God, parents, friends, the boss, the stars) for our problems.

Each of us must accept responsibility for his condition and agree with God that all have sinned and come short of the glory of God. So long as we blame others for our problems and mistakes, and so long as we disagree with God, we will never find freedom and salvation.

God is the Creator; He is able to make something out of nothing. He did that in my life, and He will do it for you. The Creator wants to give new life, new purpose, new meaning. No one is beyond hope. God is personal. The Bible teaches that God grieves and cares; He loves people but hates sin. God hears and provides. All these demonstrate His personality.

Salvation is the result of meeting the Creator personally. The Bible refers to this as being "born again." Much is printed today about being "born again," and, while millions have found the answer, millions more have not. What really is the new birth? This is not a new term; it has been around nearly two thousand years. It came from the lips of Jesus while He was addressing one of the most devout and religious men of His day. Jesus spoke very plainly, "Verily, verily, I say unto thee, except a man be born again, he cannot see the kingdom of God" (John 3:3). To understand what the new birth is, we may begin by looking at what it is not.

It is not *grand resolutions, New Year's promises,* or *self-effort.* I remember standing at the grave of one of my best high school friends and making a lot of resolutions about changing my lifestyle, but the next day I was back at it.

It is not being sorry for your wrongdoing. After all, everyone feels some remorse.

It is not joining the church. I was talking to a very successful businessman on an airplane. My heart ached when he told me, "I am a church member. I don't need to be born again." Religion is not the new birth. You can be baptized, dunked, christened, sprinkled, splashed, and squirted and still not be born again. If you could earn forgiveness and eternal life by being sincere or becoming a church member, then Jesus never would have had to be crucified.

The new birth is:

1) *A spiritual birth.* Read John 3:1–7. Our first birth was involuntary; we had nothing to say about it. The new birth is strictly voluntary; we have a choice. Our physical birth was of the flesh, meaning that our life ends at death. The new birth is of the spirit and gives eternal life. It is a means of joining God's forever family.

2) *Personal.* Salvation is not a corporate plan, and it does not happen by osmosis. You believe in God?

Fine. The Bible says, "... The devils also believe, and tremble" (James 2:19). Believing in Jesus as Savior is not complete until you allow Him to become your personal Savior.

3) *An imperative.* Jesus said you *must* be born again. He didn't say only the most evil, or if it is convenient, or if it is permissible with your denomination. He said, "... Except a man be born again, he cannot *see* the kingdom of God" (John 3:3, italics mine).

4) *Powerful.* It is a life-changing, life-saving experience. It is inviting the Son of God to live in your life. It is being a child of God instead of remaining a child of Satan. It is passing from spiritual death into spiritual life. Instead of spending eternity apart from God, you spend it with Him in heaven. He is waiting for you to accept this free gift and invite Him into your life. (See John 1:12; Rev. 3:20; Rom. 10:9, 13.)

The greatest provision you can make for your family is providing them an example. The new birth makes it possible for you to be equipped and ready for the privileged responsibility of being a parent. Many parents know they ought to make peace with God, but they wait. They may send their children to church, hoping to help their children while their own lives cancel out much of what the kids learn at church. One ounce of parents is worth a pound of clergy.

The Word of God plainly teaches that parents are responsible for their children and that being a parent is a twenty-four-hour-a-day job. "And thou shalt teach them diligently unto thy children [the laws and commandments of God], and shalt talk of them when thou sittest in thine house, and when thou walkest by the way, and when thou liest down, and when thou risest up" (Deut. 6:7).

Preparing our children for life means we must equip them with knowledge that will keep them from destroying their lives. To protect our children we must train them in the Word of God. This is done in two ways: One is for the family to be faithful to the church. There is no substitute for the church. In Luke 4:16 we read that Jesus "...came to Nazareth, where he had been brought up: and, as his custom was, he went into the synagogue on the sabbath day...." In Hebrews 10:25 the Bible urges that we not forsake "...the assembling of ourselves together, as the manner of some is..." The church is the family's best friend.

Being faithful to the church should include participation in worship services, as well as in other social, recreational, educational, and special services available from time to time. Make sure, however, that it is the right kind of church—a church that believes and teaches the Bible as the inspired Word of God, believes in the deity of Christ, His virgin birth, His atonement and bodily resurrection, His miracles, salvation by grace, and the reality of heaven and hell. Don't join a certain church just because you were brought up in it. Look for a church that preaches and teaches the Bible, a place where people are being saved, a church with an active and consecrated program for your youth.

Perhaps in no other area of life can a father be so great an example to his children than his role as an active member of a church. Children can see through facades. If you place high value on the church, you will be faithful in attendance, giving, and service.

But most parents love the pillow istead of the pew, or are weekend nature lovers. Don't join a church the same way you join a club. Membership in a church is like membership in a family.

The other way to train your children is by having a family altar. An altar is a place of sacrifice and worship. There should be a time set apart daily for the family to be together for fun, help with school work, Bible stories, and prayers. If you don't begin this while the children are young, don't expect them to be around for it when they are teens. This is where family problems can be solved through communication, prayer, and Bible study. This will meet their needs for love, affection, discipline, and training by example. It is here you can share each other's burdens. Parents should share some burdens with their children and vice versa. Pray for each other, whether it be for help in a ballgame, a test, a date, or an illness. A family altar will alter your family.

Dr. C. S. Lovett said, "If we have been faithful, consistent, and firm the first twelve years of their lives, there is quite a package of truth of work in their lives. And when they receive Christ, they are equipped with a new nature and the Holy Spirit has access to his will. Then the child will be able with God's help to overcome the temptations and pressures of sex, crime, drugs, alcohol, etc."[7]

In addition to preventing their children from crashing over the cliff, parents must get involved in church, school and community projects to help those who have already gone over the edge.

Spirituality is the eternal glue that holds families together. Take advantage of God-given opportunities.

What Do You Think?

1. Give your definition of a home. What can you personally do to contribute to that definition and make it a reality?
2. Name those conditions in your home that are beyond your control and decide how to live with and handle them.
3. What would you change about your home and family if you could? What do you think your parent(s) would change about you?
4. Discuss what you feel is effective discipline for a teen-ager. How should parents decide on a punishment to fit the offense? Should punishments be preset as a warning?
5. Why do parents and teens have problems communicating? How could this be improved?
6. You claim you are not a child anymore, that you are mature enough to make some decisions on your own. How can you prove this to your parents? What kind of responsibilities can you undertake in the home as well as outside the home?
7. List at least ten adventurous options a family can undertake in offering a teen an alternative to the temporary thrills of drug using. Be realistic in keeping down expenses and be prepared to take much of the responsiblity for the planning.
8. Name at least two important things a family can do to equip the teen-ager to resist the pressure of the crowd.

9.

The Response of the Church

CHURCH, WAKE UP!

IN THIS AGE, WHICH MANY BIBLE students believe to be the last days when perilous times and dangerous times shall come, it seems the church should wake up.

In this age when millions of our children are turning to drugs, when venereal disease is spreading like an epidemic, when teens rank as the second highest age group in suicide statistics, when over a million teens run away and thousands walk away from home unnoticed, when over a million teen-age girls are pregnant, it seems the church should wake up.

In this age of a half-million legal abortions among teens and an estimated half-million illegal ones; when over six-hundred million dollars' worth of damage is inflicted on public schools by students; when over seventy thousand school teachers are assaulted by their students; when the FBI reports that two-thirds of all violent crime (murder, rape, assault) is committed by those under the age of twenty-one and 50 percent by those under the age of eighteen; when juvenile crime has increased 245 percent in the last thirteen years, it seems the church should wake up.

In this age when billions of dollars' worth of

merchandise is stolen by teens; when operation of the juvenile court system is costing twelve billion dollars a year nationwide; when the bang of the divorce court gavel is louder than the ring of wedding bells, as two million homes and more are breaking up; when millions of teens are turning to sexual perversion and homosexuality; when millions of teens are roaming the streets like zombies, confused, lonely, empty, and bored, ready to do almost anything for a thrill, it would seem the church should wake up.

I believe the church ought to be the greatest force in every community, especially in rescuing the youth of America and their families from the roaring lion. There is nothing more exciting than a church that is truly alive, reaching a community with the life-changing, life-saving message of Jesus Christ. On the other hand, there is nothing more pathetic than a church that offers only a cold, dead religion.

The church I refer to is not a building. It is people. A local congregation. A family. Many churches have forgotten their motivation, their mission, their message, and consequently they have forfeited their miracles. There is a tremendous discrepancy between the church as pictured in the New Testament and the church of today. The first-century church was accused of "turning the world upside down," but today, far too often, it is a sleeping giant. The church as pictured in the pages of the Book of Acts was an active force, reaching out in love with outstretched arms. Many churches today are sitting back with their arms folded, telling he world, "We're satisfied."

If people can't turn to the church for help, where can they turn? The world believes the influence of most churches is declining. Read the words of a leading educational executive: "So much of society's responsibility in raising children has shifted to the schools. For increasing numbers of youth, the church and family have ceased to play significant roles" (Terry Herndon, former executive director of the National Education Association).

The church must respond, and refusal to do so is spiritual and social treason. The word "apathy" is actually a medical term stemming from the Greek word *apatheia*, which means "no feeling." The Greeks used *apatheia* to describe their idea of a characteristic of gods. Two thousand years ago the Greeks believed god was *apatheia*; he had no ability to feel. They reasoned that if god could feel joy, sorrow, or anger, then lowly, insignificant man could affect or move god. To the Greek mind, god was above caring about worthless man. For this reason, the apostle Paul wrote in 1 Corinthians 1:18 to the Greeks in Corinth, "The preaching of the cross is to them that perish foolishness; but unto us which are saved it is the power of God."

The Greeks' belief resembles the Hindu mythology with its cast of 330 million gods, with devotees worshiping stone images, statues, and idols of the gods. Those figures have no eyes to see with, no mouths to speak with, no brains to think with, and no hearts to love with.

This illustrates the main difference between Christianity and all other religions. While the others teach that man must desperately try to find God, offering gifts of sacrifice in an attempt to reach up to Him, Christianity teaches that God reaches down to man through His Son. The Bible is God's revelation to man, in which He reveals Himself as a loving heavenly Father who sees, loves, cares, and is capable of anger. Jesus Christ, as God in the flesh, often wept over man. Very simply, the Greeks felt God was above involvement in human affairs, yet Christians believe that the one and only true God cared so much that He became flesh. Therefore, if a church refuses to respond, to get involved, and to feel and care, then it is apatheia—dead—or it is the pagan temple of a false god.

The Motivation for the Response

The response of the church should be motivated by several factors. First, there is the condition of modern man. Man is a restless creature and often out of control. Drugs, disease, and drunkenness are only the symptoms of a deadly disease called sin. Man is a sinner and rebel who is constantly offending and rebelling against a loving and holy God. The Bible plainly teaches that man is a sinner by nature (Ps. 51:5), by practice (John 3:19), and by choice (John 3:17,18). This sin is like the chronic disease, leprosy, caused by a microorganism that destroys nerve endings. Sin eventually destroys one's ability to perceive the tragedy of spiritual death. The church is the only institution entrusted with the cure for this otherwise fatal disease.

The second motivation for the church today is the receptiveness of man. These, for me, are even more exciting days of opportunity than the day of Pentecost. Both young and old have never been more open to the claims of Christ. While it is true that evil is more rampant than ever, that drugs, booze, sex, and false cults are leaving people burned out and empty, people are nevertheless open to Jesus. In the words of a famous rock star I shared my faith with, "Man, I've tried everything and I'm still bored, empty, and sick." Futility can open the mind and make it responsive to the message of Jesus. Recently, I have found in my crusades greater response to the gospel than ever before.

The third motivation for the church's response is the consequence of failing to rescue individuals from the roaring lion. Millions of teens will be destroyed and devoured, and those not destroyed will go through life scarred. Empty teen-agers grow into empty adults. Have you ever talked to a young man or young woman who had just violated a moral standard he or she believed in? Because of one night of drugs or alcohol they are crushed, left feeling dirty, guilty, and empty. Tragically, this often leads to more drugs or booze in an effort to forget or to masquerade the sin.

The consequences of our lack of response are frightening. Every time I counsel a disenchanted teen or a little girl in trouble, or help to scrape a teen up off the streets after a drug- or alcohol-related accident, I vow to work even harder to destroy that roaring lion. There is nothing but a hell-on-earth existence for many teens, and even death offers no escape, for then comes the Judgement and, for most, eternal separation from God.

The church's fourth motivation is the urgency of the hour. I believe that these are the last days; the final curtain is about to fall; it's the fourth quarter; the sun is about to sink in the West. The feeling that man hasn't long to go is echoed by scientists, historians, and the clergy. This is evidenced by the "boom of doom" shelves in bookstores crammed with predictions of the destruction of the human race. The Bible plainly teaches over three hundred times in the New Testament that Jesus Christ is coming again, and I believe He is coming soon. The churches most effective in rescuing people are those working as if this is the last day we have to reach people for Jesus. Surely the church must wake up and work while it is still day, because "the night cometh, when no man can work" (John 9:4).

Finally, our primary motivation is obedience to the divine mandate of Jesus Christ. Jesus had but one mission: to seek and to save the lost. Jesus, addressing God, said of His disciples in John 17:18, "As thou hast sent me into the world, even so have I also sent them into the world." It was the plan and purpose of Jesus to use His disciples to win the world to Himself. The Bible teaches that Jesus instituted the church for this purpose. He intended for the church to perform other tasks of service, but its supreme objective is to bring lost men, women, children, and teens to Christ. The New Testament does not separate evangelism from other functions of the church. Evangelism *is* the church, and that church which ceases to evangelize is neglecting its primary reason for being. When the church ceases to thrive, it begins to die.

Upon founding the church, Jesus said His true church would be the greatest asset of any community because of its aggessive assault on hell itself. He said, ". . . Upon this rock I will build my church; and the gates of hell shall not prevail against it" (Matt. 16:18). To understand and interpret this statement accurately, we must define the key word "prevail." There are those who think the word indicates that the gates of hell are on the offense, while the church is playing defense, trying desperately to hang on. They say no matter how strong evil becomes in the world, the church will never be destroyed by it.

However, the word "prevail" is a compound Greek

word made up of the words "strength" and "against." Therefore, "prevail" means "strength against." So Jesus put the church of the living God on the offense and the gates of hell on the defense. Literally, the gates of hell will not have strength enough to stand against the power and strength of the church. No power in the universe can stop God's church.

The Message of Response

A capsule definition of Christianity, and therefore the message of the church, is given by the apostle Paul in 1 Corinthians 15:3–8: "... Christ died for our sins according to the scriptures; and that he was buried, and that he rose again the third day according to the scriptures; and that he was seen of Cephas, then of the twelve ..." In these confusing days God has given this plumbline to keep us true and straight. Our message consists of: 1) the person and work of Jesus Christ; 2) the nature of man; and 3) the authority of the Scriptures.

True preaching is the proclamation of the story of Jesus Christ. Who is Jesus Christ? He is the eternal Son of God, born of a virgin, One who lived a sinless life and then became our Substitute and paid for our sins. The work of Christ was His sacrificial death, called the Atonement, and His supernatural bodily resurrection. Yesterday He *died* for me; today He *lives* for me; tomorrow He *comes* for me.

True preaching is the proclamation of the nature of man. The Cross of Jesus Christ proves we are guilty sinners. The Cross of Jesus demonstrates the love of God in that "God so loved the world, that he gave his only begotten Son, that whosoever believeth in him should not perish, but have everlasting life" (John 3:16). The Cross of Jesus also demonstrates the holiness of God. God must punish sin. The Cross reveals the true, sinful nature of man, which is constantly rebelling and offending the holiness of God.

True preaching of the Cross demands repentance. This was the message of the prophets of old, of John the Baptist, of the Lord Jesus Himself, and of the apostles. Man must turn around, because man by choice has turned his back on God. The reason people get into trouble in their relationships with God and with others is because of their sinful natures. Every man is a sinner. To preach against sin is to offer hope. When a homosexual, a drunkard, or a drug addict is told he is "sick," he is condemned; but label his disease "sin," as God does, and you offer him hope. The message of the Cross offers the hope, "You don't have to stay the way you are." "Therefore if any man be in Christ, he is a new creature: old things are passed away; behold, all things are become new" (2 Cor. 5:17).

True preaching is based on the authority of the Bible. Preaching is the proclamation of the Good News of salvation from God through man to men. The man and the message are two essential elements.

The man God calls to preach the riches of Jesus Christ the Lord should be a converted man. The business of a Christian minister is to specialize in spiritual problems; therefore, he must be a spiritual being, one who has been born again of the Spirit. An unconverted or an unregenerated man is dead in trespasses and sin (Eph. 2:1) and is therefore spiritually dead. His understanding has been darkened, and he is alienated from the life of God (Eph. 4:18). It is fraud for an unconverted man to be about spiritual business. The great Charles Spurgeon once said,

"How horrible to be a preacher of the Gospel and yet to be unconverted! Let each man here whisper to his own inmost soul, 'What a dreadful thing it will be for me if I should be ignorant of the power of the truth which I am preparing to proclaim!' "[1]

A preacher of the truth must be a consecrated man. The Latin word *consecrare* means to make holy. Our life must be a set-apart, dedicated life. In every relationship, in every obligation, in every season it must be said about us as it was said about Elisha, ". . . Behold now, I perceive that this is an holy man of God, which passeth by us continually" (2 Kings 4:9). We hear a great deal about our physical health, but the biblical word for spiritual health is holiness.

The man called by God to preach must also be a committed man—committed to his Lord, his family, and his congregation. He must also be committed to the Word of God, the Bible. Our generation is perishing for lack of truth, and the source of truth is the Word of God. The Word of God is powerful. It has power to convict of sin, to convert, to cleanse from sin. "I am not ashamed of the gospel of Christ: for it is the power of God unto salvation to every one that believeth; to the Jew first, and also to the Greek" (Rom. 1:16). The Greek word for power is *dunamis*, which gives us the word "dynamite" (read also Hebrews 4:12,13).

The truth of God is precious. The Word of God is like a valuable, highly prized gem. It must be handled delicately, guarded even as a rare emerald or diamond is guarded. The apostle Paul warned Timothy to "study to shew thyself approved unto God, a workman that needeth not to be ashamed, rightly dividing the word of truth" (2 Tim. 2:15). "Rightly dividing" means to handle carefully and to cut straight, as a jeweler cuts a precious stone, with great care. A true preacher of the Gospel will build up the Bible and defend the faith, not undermine it and cut the heart out of it. Those who undermine the Bible reveal their own problems, not God's.

Too many preachers, in an effort to masquerade as scholars, have been offering stones instead of bread to their people. It is obvious that something is wrong. We teach young people in our churches from the cradle roll until college and career age. Shortly after they leave to attend colleges or liberal denominational schools, their faith is often shattered. Why? Can it be because they have not received what they need in order to ground them in the truths of the Bible? Then when liberal professors, the cults, Eastern religions, mysticism, and philosophies try to discredit the Word, they become confused.

As I travel, I find a spiritual famine among young people. When questioned about their biblical illiteracy, the young people sadly answer, "Oh, I had a preacher (Sunday School teacher, parent, professor) who told me most of the Bible is the work of man." We should remember that since the beginning of the world Satan's main assault on the Scriptures has been, "Did God really say it?" Any effort by any person to undermine the authority of the Word of God marks him as an enemy of the Cross. I believe our message should be built on the authority of the Scriptures. Over three thousand times in the Old Testatment alone the Bible says, "Thus saith the Lord God," "God said," or "The Word of the Lord came."

A true preacher must be committed to the Word of God and should teach anyone who will listen. The Word can be trusted; you can build a family, a life, an eternity on the Word of God. Young people need to be assured that the Bible is a road map and a compass. Many preachers are trying to feed giraffes, instead of sheep, by preaching way over the heads of their congregations. Jesus should be our pattern, and it was written that "... the common people heard him gladly" (Mark 12:37). In these confusing days, we need a certain voice. Paul said, "If the trumpet give an uncertain sound, who shall prepare himself to the battle?" (1 Cor. 14:8).

When one preaches the Resurrection, he is preaching hope. I always preach messages of hope to let people know God cares (1 Pet. 5:7; Isa. 1:18; Matt. 11:28–30). God's Word causes a desire for change. It changes desires and appetites. The Word also comforts. I agree with Aelred Graham who said, "The preacher of the Gospel must be ready to afflict the comfortable as well as comfort the afflicted."[2]

Methods for Our Response

All these methods are based on sound biblical principles because methods often change, but biblical principle never changes. Pastors, staff workers, Sunday School workers, and youth workers should prayerfully take inventory of their lives and methods.

1) *Our Foundation*—"If the foundations be destroyed, what can the righteous do?" (Ps. 11:3). Our entire foundation and authority to minister is our relationship to Jesus Christ and our relationship to our families. We will never be effective in persuading others to receive the abundant life through Christ unless we have an abundant life personally and corporately with our families.

2) *Be a Priest*—We are to be people of prayer, because we are fighting spiritual wars that will never be won in the flesh. We are commanded to intercede

for others in the presence of our holy God. Stay prayed up. Preaching, singing, teaching, and counseling without much prayer are just sounding brass and tinkling cymbals. We must stay prayed up, because we only have one or two hours a week to change the lives of teens who have been listening to other influences much of the time. We must have the attitude of the early Christians—a combination of humility and boldness. Without prayer, there will not be the supernatural touch of God.

3) *Be a Prophet*—A prophet is a person so close to the heart of God that he knows the mind of God and shares it with people in language they can understand. Bookstore sermons are not good enough. The tragedy of these last days is that we have too many dead preachers giving out dead sermons to dead people. The phrase "in a language they can understand" needs to be the motto for those who have the responsibility of teaching the most important Book in the world. Preachers and teachers should sit down with their young people and ask them outright, "Do I come across? Am I boring?" Then they need to ask themselves: Do the kids like me as a person? Do they know I love them? It is not hard to understand why 80 percent of non-Christians never darken the doors of a church. Too many services are dull, dreary, and dead. Some of them sound like funerals. The preacher, the teachers, the song leader, and the choir need to catch on fire. Joy is the fruit of the presence of God.

4) *Be a Parent and Partner*—Many people in Christian service are too busy for their families and mates. Don't be one of those who is running around trying to save everybody else's kids while losing his own. Be available to your own family.

5) *Be Alive*—In order to convince teens that Jesus gives real life, you must live the real life. Don't be afraid to have teens in your home, especially in this age of divorce and separation. Young people need to see that Jesus makes a difference in the home. Be the positive example kids are looking for. Be turned on to life; be fun to be around.

6) *Love Your Youth*—The youth director should not become just a spiritual baby-sitter. Visit in the homes of the young people and see their real needs. Pray for them by name. A teen-ager will never share his problem with someone who doesn't take a personal interest in him.

7) *Advertise That You Care*—A compassionate young pastor I know devotes two hours every Thursday after school to just teens. He offers refreshments and time just for them. He calls it "I care." One pastor said, "There are two groups of people I never trust to anyone else: my men and my teens."

8) *Be Yourself*—There are those who mistakenly believe you must be an ex-drug addict to counsel teens about drugs. Many times, adults are frustrated by their inability to communicate with the young so they try to imitate the young. Young people searching for answers are not looking for someone just like themselves. They are looking for a fresh face, for someone different. Physical appearance is important, because first impressions are formed by it. Be fashionable, well-groomed, and neat. But don't try to be "groovier than thou."

9) *Be Masculine or Feminine*—In this age of sex role confusion, there should be clear-cut role models in our churches. Effeminate men or bossy women can destroy a church youth program.

10) *Have Good Music*—In our desperation to reach

kids, we have tried to compete with the world in music. We have dragged in rock-and-roll music and injected it with Christian words. There is no such thing as "Jesus rock." Rock music is rock music. Mini-rock concerts may pack a house for one night, but there aren't many spiritual results afterward. Searching kids are looking for peace, even in music. Don't offer them the same thing they are trying to escape from. We need to give our teens a rock that doesn't roll—the Rock of Ages.

11) *Don't Fool Yourself*—Don't pretend you have a great bunch of kids just because they are at the Sunday morning services. Most are forced to be there by their parents. Some of them sit so far back in the church that by the time they hear the sermon it's only a rumor. Be honest in your evaluation of the youth scene in your church.

12) *Stay in Touch*—Be seen with kids at school, games, and where they congregate. To be in touch you must leave your office or church and go where they are. Eighty percent of their waking hours are spent at school or in school-related activities. As a pastor and an associate pastor, I ate lunch with my youth group at school, and I systematically took each of my kids out for a Coke and a rap session. At ball games I sat with the kids. We often held after-glow sessions in our homes. As a result, I was known as a pastor who cared about kids.

13) *Make Them Feel Welcome*—The attraction of rock concerts for teens offers us great insight. They feel comfortable with their peers. At home they have to put on an act and attempt to live up to what they know adults expect. I often felt the uneasiness of church members when I came in with long hair; I felt they were speculating about my reputation. I felt

dirty and out of place. Yet, when we look at the life of Jesus, we see that sinners felt loved and welcomed by Him. Educate older members that there is no place for power struggles, old grudges, or personal opinions based on prejudice or preconceived ideas about young people. Teach your young people to avoid destructive cliques. Instruct your church on how to make everyone feel welcome. Remind the members of Jesus' treatment of those considered different.

14) *Avoid Every Appearance of Evil*—I have found it helpful to remain above reproach in testimony, and, therefore, I never counsel a girl or woman while alone. My wife or another lady in the church may counsel a young girl better than I can, anyway. I do counsel young girls and women when we can be seen but not heard by others (in the middle of a church auditorium, for example).

15) *Develop a Total Youth Program*—Too many churches condemn their young people for the things they do and the places they go without providing alternatives. Avoid having a lopsided ministry. For several years I made the mistake of only providing discipleship and soulwinning without recreation or social events.

16) *Prayerfully Select Youth Workers*—I know churches that have been set back several years because they placed the wrong adults in the youth department. It is obvious that youth workers need to be born again, but they should also have a radiant Christian life and be faithful to the church, ministry, and staff. It is amazing how many churches will stick any warm body in to work with teens. Every church owes it to the Lord, to its members, and to its community to hire the best youth workers possible. These people must love kids and have time for them.

17) *Teach in Exciting Ways*—Teaching is a powerful tool. Communists know it, as do liberals and atheists. I believe the rioting and rebellion on college campuses in the late sixties was the result of radical and liberal professors. It is known to those who keep abreast of the educational system that some of the most powerful and influential teachers in America are atheists.

When a Communist nation takes over another country (for example, in Vietnam and Cuba), all the teachers are removed from the educational system and Communist teachers are installed to indoctrinate children and youth, the leaders of tomorrow. There is one man, who, though now dead, still has considerable influence over eight hundred million people, one fifth of the population of the world, and who had hoped to control the rest. He didn't have a Ph.D., but he knew the power of teaching. His book is called *The Little Red Book, The Quotations of Mao Tse Tung.*

We must teach the world the sayings of Jesus with authoritative, anointed teachers. Sunday should be the most exciting day of the week.

18) *Use Sound and Good Material*—In many churches, material taught in Sunday School and church training are still written for the mentality of another generation. If your denomination or convention does not print sound and interesting material, look elsewhere. Be aware that much liberal teaching material is being foisted off on churches.

19) *Use Tapes and Books*—Available to you are tapes and books on dating, sex, knowing God's will, and subjects of particular interest to youth by some of today's greatest speakers and writers.

20) *Meet Their Needs without Spoiling Them*—Provide

for teens and make every effort to meet their needs, but don't set them up on pedestals. Today the danger exists that we "worship" at the shrine of youth. Remember, an eighteen-year-old boy must be saved the same way an eighty-year-old man or an eight-year-old boy must be saved. Make sure you give them the bread and water of life instead of Kool-Aid and cookies, because the devil has a "party" for them that will blow the tops of their heads off. Plan special events and bring in top youth speakers and singers. Combine forces with other churches, and do it right.

There's one last thing to remember: The greatest thing you can do for a young person is to win his parents to Jesus.

What Do You Think?

1. Is it important to attend church? Can you worship on your own just as well? Give biblical evidence to support your claim.
2. Who began the church and for what purpose?
3. Is the Bible the Word of God? Based on 2 Timothy 3:16, can we find the answers to life in the Bible?
4. What can you do personally to make your church or youth group a more effective minister to teenagers who use drugs? What can your youth group do as a whole?
5. List ten activities your church or youth group can sponsor to help teen-agers say "No" to peer pressure. What type of activities or ministry will help them to continue to say "no" to following the crowd?
6. Make an appointment with your pastor, youth

pastor, or Sunday school worker. Get to know them; let them get to know you. Share your needs and pray together. Then, using what you have learned from this time, meet with someone else and attempt to minister to them in the same way you have been ministered to.

10.

The Response of the School

REFERENCE HAS ALREADY BEEN MADE in Chapter 1 to the fact that America's three great pillars are crumbling and failing to fulfill the task for which they were created. These three pillars—the home, the church, and the school—form our foundation. It is in this order that they were established, and each is dependent upon the other. The result of this failure ensures the destruction of our nation's foundation.

The subject of the public schools is one of the most widley discussed topics in America. From the simple masses to the sophisticated media, all are anxious to contribute their opinions. It is understandable that society has high expectations and standards for the public schools, since it has entrusted two of its most cherished possessions—its children and its future—to the care of the schools.

Education has become an important function of state and local government. This is evidenced by the compulsory school attendance laws and the great expenditure of public funds for schools.

At this critical time in our nation's history, it is imperative that we are not deceived by all the talk of peace in our public schools. There is no peace. On the surface, things appear to be calm in comparison to the riots and organized protests of the late sixties. But underneath the thin veneer there lies a volcano about to erupt. This is written in the spirit of concern rather than of condemnation.

In order to understand why our schools have been called "prisons" by students and "blackboard jungles" by teachers, let us examine three areas of concern: the crisis, the curriculum, and the cultivators.

THE CRISIS

Without trying to draw an overly depressing portrait of our public schools, we must expose the crisis. This crisis is brought about by three factors: violence, drugs, and lack of discipline.

Violence has turned our schools into "blackboard jungles" and "battle zones," and students and teachers alike suffer from combat neurosis. In 1984 President Reagan urged Americans to help teachers regain control of their classrooms, stating that public schools are filled with unruly behavior and even violence. He cited a report by the National Institute of Education as saying that each month three million secondary schoolchildren were victims of crime. "Each month, some 2.5 million students were victims of robberies and thefts and more than 250,000 students suffered physical attacks. In large cities, the problem was so bad that almost 8 percent of urban junior and senior high school students missed at least one day in the classroom per month because they were afraid to go to school," he said. The president further stated that each month six thousand teachers are robbed, one hundred twenty-five thousand are threatened with physical harm, and at least one thousand are assaulted so severely they require medical care. He added: "But we can't get learning back into our schools until we get the crime and violence out. Find out what you can do to help. By working together, we can restore good order to America's classrooms and give our sons and daughters the education they deserve."[1]

These young offenders are obviously restless, angry, and bored, venting their frustration and anger on fellow students, teachers, and school buildings. In one year, over six hundred million dollars' worth of damage was inflicted by students to their own school buildings. This is more than is spent on new textbooks in a year. This is the reason Joseph Califano, former secretary of Health, Education and Welfare, has said, "The most dangerous place for a child to be is in school."

Most educators agree that to get to the root of school violence several changes are essential: 1) Smaller schools and smaller classes, or a "schools within schools" concept. In larger schools, this would allow more personal attention for students. 2) Curriculum reform, with instruction in practical skills to make education "more relevent" for students of all backgrounds. 3) Strong principals with firm, fair, consistent systems of discipline. 4) A joint effort between society and the schools.

Lack of discipline has given birth to the epidemic of violence and drug abuse in our schools. The control of many of our schools has been transferred from teacher and administrator to parent and student. Many believe that this breakdown began in 1957 when a Detroit youth, a discipline problem, was paddled. A lawsuit over the rights of students followed and shook the educational empire to its foundation. Instead of maintaining the status quo by holding the line on discipline in the classrooms and schools, educational leaders surrendered and changed their disciplinary tactics. This was a major victory for violent and unruly students.

Finally, in the due process of law, the case passed through the courts and years later appeared on the docket of the Supreme Court. During this time, the power of the teacher had deteriorated. The Supreme Court reached the following verdict: The rights of the youth had not been violated; the school authorities had been within their rights in disciplining the youth. Simply stated, corporal punishment was found to be a legal means of student discipline.

For years, Americans have regarded the lack of discipline as the biggest problem facing public schools, according to the Gallup Poll of Public Opinion Toward Education. There is no time to learn when classroom time must be spent on discipline. The crises of drugs and violence could be greatly diminished if administrations would support teachers in discipline. Fear is the demon that is driving teachers to psychiatrists, to pills, to the bottle, and finally to other occupations. Teachers fear the violent student, the administration that fails to support, the school board, and the PTA. Principals have their own fears. Many refuse to admit there is a problem, for fear of being labeled incompetent. Superintendents often lie to the school boards, and school boards lie to the communities. Teachers, principals, administrators, superintendents, school boards, and parents have lost control in many of our schools.

Discipline in the school means instruction, correction, teaching, training, the molding of moral character and mental faculties. Without discipline, there is no learning or self-control. It is ironic that parents who do not care enough about their children to discipline them are the first to yell "lawsuit" if the school administration is forced to discipline their children.

Our present crisis in the classroom can also be traced to the drug scene. Reference was made in Chapter 1 to the availability of drugs on the public school campus, in the parking lot, or at the youth hangout. It seems reasonable to demand that trafficking and usage of illegal drugs not be permitted on public school grounds. The decision to take drugs is not rational, but emotional. Any psychological or physical dependence on drugs is diametrically opposed to the goals of the educational process.

Sidney Cohen, in *The Drug Dilemma*, has said:

If the educator is to learn anything from the current striving for drug-induced perceptual, emotional, and cognitive changes, it is that important areas of human experience have been neglected by our child-rearing and child-teaching practices. Many of those who are attracted to the drug experience suffer from anhedonism, the inability to derive pleasure from ordinary existence, and alienation, the inability to find meaning within or without oneself. These are serious deficits, and in a young person they lead to serious disorders of behavior or character. From childhood through adolescence we are failing (1) to produce goals appropriate to our times, (2) to train the emotions and the senses, and (3) to set limits. Therefore, goallessness, an inability to enjoy, and an attenuated sense of social responsibility predispose to chemical escape, chemical hedonism, and the search for chemical enlightenment. The drug abuse problem in our schools is not only shocking, and increasing; it is increasing in progressively younger age groups, even to elementary school age children.[2]

THE CURRICULUM

The curriculum taught in the public schools is cause for concern. The Parent-Teachers Association

(PTA) voices concern on the part of parents who feel that the basic skills of reading, writing, and arithmetic are lacking in students of all ages. Many of the materials used are blasphemous, obscene, left-wing, and non-patriotic, claim a number of parents. Many educators and students find the materials obsolete and irrelevant.

More Americans are spending more time in formal education than ever before. Two out of three adults are high-school graduates, and one out of seven holds a college degree. Although the statistics appear to show that Americans are now better educated, the opposite is actually true. Unfortunately, it seems the amount of time spent in classrooms does not relate directly to the level of student knowledge. Of course, there are many factors involved here, but there is a major gap between formal education and training and acutal education and learning.

In an effort to be informal and innovative, public educators have abandoned many traditions. This, in turn, has caused a mass exodus to the private schools. It should be obvious that the outbreak of parent-teacher disputes and the trend toward establishment of conservative alternative schools (whether secular or Christian) are signs of public mistrust and concern.

Many educators try to pass the new private schools off as efforts to avoid racial integration. While this may be true in some cases, most alternative schools stress conservative American values; this is what parents want for their children. The curriculum of these schools generally includes the basic "three Rs" and also promotes character building, discipline, patriotism, and Bible reading. Poor curriculum and lack of student interest go hand in hand. The time has come to end tinkering with traditional values and to put away the teaching reforms that have gone sour. It is my belief that education today must include a new set of three Rs: respect, restraint, and responsibility. Could these be the reasons most private schools have waiting lists?

The battle to determine curriculum could be labeled "the battle for the mind." I realize that curriculum reform movements have been going strong since the mid-1920s, when school administrators took up the gospel of "progressive education" form John Dewey. Liberal, humanist teaching marches on, and parents simply cannot allow this one-sided education to continue, especially when young and impressionable self-images are at stake. Recent research indicates there is no single factor more important to a youngster's social development than his self-image. A major psychological tenet is that when we lose respect for ourselves, we lose respect for others.

Many mental, emotional, and spiritual bombs are being dropped on our young away from school, but two exploding in classrooms are among the most crippling and confusing.

The first of these is Darwin's theory of evolution, which in many schools is taught as fact. This theory maintains that all creatures, including man, evolved from lower forms of life after millennia of competition in the battle of the fittest. This fight for survival is called "natural selection." This theory suggests that man is animalistic in origin and at death merely returns to dust. The underlying idea is that man is an accident of nature, a highly developed animal, merely dust in the wind, and that, as such, he might as well act like an animal. He has no special origin, no special particular purpose, and no sure destiny.

The second mental bomb exploding on young,

formative minds is the teaching of Sigmund Freud. Freud, the father of psychoanalysis, was an atheist who embraced Darwin's concept of the origin of man. Boris Sokoloff gives us great insight into Freud's doctrines in the book *Permissive Society*. "Freud's doctrines included that man has no special purpose on this earth, no purpose for man's existence, there is no goal and no God. Therefore all is permitted."[3]

Freud provided the foundation for today's permissive society by teaching that everything is permissible and that the natural drives of man should not be repressed. Man's conscience, society, and the Bible all strongly suggest otherwise. Freud's obsession with sex was not his only crippling blow to the self-image. He also gave man a built-in alibi when he taught that we are not responsible for own behavior because it is a result of early childhood experiences and, therefore, beyond our control or responsibility.

With one scientist telling us we originated as an amoeba and a doctor proclaiming man as a high order of animal not responsible for his own actions, it is no wonder we have a generation of confused, restless, bored, young people. We have much to unlearn, and it is obvious there is a missing dimension in our educational system.

It seems that modern education has failed to provide the worthwhile goals and values that inspire youth to discipline themselves in preparation for the challenges of personal or public crisis. The curriculum used in our modern schools should equip students to meet life head-on with respect, responsibility, and restraint. They should be so thoroughly equipped that, even though they cannot solve every problem by themselves, they will know where they can find solutions. There must be an effort to eradicate the one-sided education that fails to answer life's most important questions: What is man? Why is he here? Where is he headed? What is man's responsibility to his family, community, nation, and world? The student without such knowledge is unprepared for life itself.

Several states have passed laws requiring high-school graduates to have certain practical "life skills." They ask: Can you figure out the amount of change you should receive? Can you fill out a job application blank? Do you know how to locate information in a telephone book? Do you know how and whom to contact in case of emergencies? Can you make out and balance a family buget? Do you know how credit cards work? Do you know how to buy a house? Can you write checks and balance a checkbook? Do you know how to read a map? Are you able to read and understand road signs? Are you able to identify the cautions and warnings on product labels? It is tragic to know that many high-school graduates are unprepared to earn livings. Sadder still, many students are as unfit morally as they are mentally.

Am I proposing some new methods? A new direction in education? Just the opposite. I stand with the fundamentals of learning on which this country's educational system was founded.

We have an obligation to educate the whole man by building his character. Development of a child's ability to absorb materialistic knowledge is not enough. We must instruct, but we must also inspire. Motivation should be the Siamese twin of education. Most students spend their time learning skills with which they later accomplish very little. Teaching how to do something does not assure it will be done. Teach the *why* of doing, and students learn in spite of obstacles.

Motivation is the fire that burns the logs of knowledge they receive in education. The key is in our reason for living; this reason will keep students learning and growing.

THE CULTIVATORS

America's entire educational system, and even our country's future, depend on its teachers. The highest honor a teacher can receive is to be labeled a cultivator. A cultivator prepares soil for growth and abundance by breaking it up. The words "cultivate" and "culture" come from a root word that refers to the process of developing the intellectual and moral faculties by education. Since we place immeasurable trust in our teachers when we place our children in their classrooms, it seems only reasonable to expect cer tain qualifications of those teachers. A parent naturally wants his child's teacher to have a clear calling, to possess character, to demonstrate concern, and to be able to cultivate the children.

Response to a Call

It has been stated that more students major in education in America's colleges than in any other field. Does this choice result from a call to help shape and mold our future, or is teaching merely a vocation to fill the time until greener pastures are found? There was a time in America's history when teachers were responding to a call to have a major role in determining the future of our country.

A teacher with no goal or purpose other than receiving a paycheck is not aware of the awesome responsibility of his job. I refer to the responsibility to mold young lives. Teachers with a clear calling take advantage of the opportunity to share their knowledge with students who are in the process of making important decisions about the future. A teacher can build bridges to a child's mind that will last forever.

A teacher has the ability to influence teens more than any other adult outside the family. Since the young person's decision as to whether to use drugs stems from his attitude toward himself and the adult world, a teacher can certainly play a major role in rescuing teens from the roaring lion of drug abuse.

A teacher with a clear calling possesses clean character. Could it be that the reason our schools say they are not in the business of building character is that many teachers are not qualified to do so? Character includes attributes of moral force, integrity, and good reputation. It is frightening to see the character of some of the teachers who influence our children in the academic world and chaperone them during social functions and trips. It has been said that character is the way a man acts in the dark, when no one he knows is around to watch. A teacher's appearance, language, and attitude all reveal his character.

We expect teachers not only to equip our children with the intellectual skills necessary to earn a living, but we also expect them to instill integrity, respect, reverence, honesty, and patriotism in our children and to possess all these qualities themselves. Since, by definition, to teach means to show, to instruct, to make known by precept, example, or experience, clean character is a must for every teacher.

Another characteristic of a good teacher is concern. A concerned teacher will be alert to opportunities to help and reach out. A concerned teacher notices the child who is poorly dressed on a cold day, the child who is absent often, the child with a black eye or signs of abuse, the hyperactive or insecure child. All these children are crying for help. "Some teachers are great... they put bandages on my hurts—on my heart, on my mind, on my spirit. Those teachers cared about me, and let me know it. They gave me wings."[4]

A concerned teacher is willing to become a confidant when parents don't care or aren't able to communicate effectively. Often, teachers are the first to notice changes in behavior due to drugs. Teachers should care enough to understand, and should understand enough to take the time to learn how to help.

A teacher takes a risk in opening his heart; to do so reveals him as a real human being with feelings. Concerned teachers have been known to cry and laugh and to show other emotional qualities that lie at the very heart of real communication and teaching. The humanity of a teacher is vital if children are to learn.

Teachers who care should attempt to visit in the homes of some of their students. If they can see the neglect and abuse many students receive at home, their understanding can open the door to real learning and growing.

An outstanding teacher is one who is competent to cultivate. There is a growing concern that many young teachers share the academic deficiencies of the students. While a return to curriculum basics is a necessity, the problem cannot be solved without addressing the same lack of skills in young teachers. The goal of modern education is to make students completely prepared to withstand the battles to come. (It is better to prepare than to repair.) The educator must be equipped first in order to educate others.

I wonder if many of our dropouts aren't in reality "pushouts." A cultivator is one who teaches thinking, awakens the conscience, teaches questioning of assumptions, and helps in finding the answers. A cultivator makes "the educative process as interesting, constructive, and alive as possible."[5] This is a non-chemical way of "turning on." Ask for constructive criticism from your students. Find out if you come across clearly and if the class is enjoyable. Besides providing helpful suggestions that may improve your cultivation of young minds, this dialogue will go a long way toward establishing real trust.

Last of all, a cultivator is himself motivated and so is able to motivate others. He encourages mental growth. The poem "Gate-Crashing a Child's Life" makes this analogy: The minds of our children are as houses, owned by their souls, inhabited by instincts, wants, fears, desires, loves, hates, and happiness. The teacher can channel this freshness into his own rules and roles, or he can take the extra effort to develop these characters of the mind. Sylvia Ashton-Warner calls this "a street named variation."[6]

The role of the educator is a valuable and necessary one. He will mold lives and change nations through his work. His task should be encouraged and lightened by learning in the home, but often it is not. Taking charge of a future is an awesome responsibility, and we, as parents and friends, must stand behind the teachers with encouragement, higher pay, suggestions, love, and prayer.

What Do You Think?

1. Read carefully the statistics on crime in the schools quoted by President Reagan. Do you think these are realistic statistics that might represent the schools in your area?
2. What is the underlying cause of the lack of discipline in the schools? How do peer pressure, drug use, disrespect for parents and other factors fit in?
3. Suppose a teacher presents you with a book that is unfavorable toward Christian attitudes or that directly opposes them. How can you handle this in a mature way, keeping in mind your testimony for Christ will be involved? How would you deal with criticism in this situation?
4. What can a church do to encourage and direct students to prepare educationally for a career? Is this important?
5. Do students and their parents have the right to expect teachers to be role models? What is the responsibility of the teacher concerning moral standards? Should we look to our teachers as examples? What should determine this?
6. What can you do as an individual in your class to aid your teacher in becoming a more effective communicator to the class?

11.

How to Counsel

CHAPTER 1 WILL GIVE YOU SOME insight into the young person you are trying to counsel. You must be prepared. Scare tactics don't work anymore. Youth today are much better informed. You will need to stay informed and be aware of which drugs are popular in your community. Stay familiar with the symptoms of drug usage. You need to recognize whether the one you are counseling is in any condition to be counseled or not. Many counseling sessions or late-night confrontations between parent and teen have been wasted because the adult did not realize he was talking to a pill instead of to a person. The teen's mind must be clear before he is approached. If a person is drowning, it is not a good time to teach him to swim. Wait for a good opportunity. If you really are concerned about helping your teens or someone else's, your concern will show.

Be approachable and available. Teens must have access to you, or they will never come for help. A good opening for a talk is to ask your teen's opinions about drug-related features in the paper or on television, or to discuss a recent drug bust or a drug-related accident. Teens want and need to talk about how they feel. An opportunity may come at any time, usually after weeks and months of observation of the adult by the young person.

Counselors should also be careful of second- or third-hand information. Always consider the source, but treat information like smoke—*maybe* there is some fire. Let me remind you that there are three types of drug users: the occasional user, the thrill seeker, and the junkie. A teen-ager trying booze or pot at a weekend party is not a junkie, but his experiment is a symptom of restlessness or confusion.

THE ACTUAL SESSION

This might take place in your child's bedroom, in the living room, in a classroom after school, or in a pastor's study. The more privacy, the better.

1) Encourage the young person to face his problem squarely and honestly. Encourage him to talk about his feelings. This ventilation of pent-up feelings is a great beginning. As he shares, just *listen*. Don't condemn, but don't give false assurances such as, "Oh, you're really not that bad." Give sympathy: "I am here to help; I am on your side." Offer the hope or condolence of "You're not the first one to do this nor will you be the last." In talking with you, this may be the first time the teen has actually faced his problem. Understand that the teen is not as sure of himself as he pretends. Many teens are good at sizing up other people and manipulating them, yet they are naive about themselves.

2) He must accept his own responsibilities in this problem. Maybe he has been sinned against, or has been the victim, or has been burned, but maturity means responsibiity for your own condition. This is a biblical law as well as a social law. A fundamental assumption underlying the laws in a free society is that man is a responsible agent, that he can under-

stand and follow rules, and therefore that he can be held accountable for his own actions.

Many teens with problems will be like Adam in the Garden of Eden. They will try to cover up their shame and guilt by sewing fig leaves of excuses together. Others will avoid their parents or avoid the church, just as Adam and Eve hid themselves from the presence of God. Even after they were caught, Adam blamed the woman, and Eve blamed the serpent.

3) Ask the teen the question Jesus asked, "Wilt thou be made whole?" (John 5:6). ("Do you really want to be healed?") To a lame man who had been a cripple for thirty-eight years, it sounded like a foolish question. But people don't always want to be healed. They sometimes choose not to accept re sponsibility. Some you counsel may just want to talk about their problems or seek your sympathy. I have run across young people who, on our first meeting, have told me every minute detail of their sins. Rest assured, these are talkers who want sympathy, and they will tell anyone who will listen to their problems. Others love their sins and refuse to give them up. The Bible describes them as "lovers of pleasures more than lovers of God" (2 Tim. 3:4). By questioning them, you will be able to determine if they really want help.

4) As the teens shares, his story will probably be in bits and pieces, so be a patient listener. (Maybe that is why the Lord gave us two ears and one mouth; we need to listen twice as much as we talk!) Never push the student or teen too hard to reveal facts he isn't ready to reveal. Give him time to answer or to ask what he feels comfortable with. Be sensitive to signals of nervousness, irritability, or

boredom. Every person wants to feel important and wanted.

Many times as I hear problems, the young person comments, "You are the first person who has ever listened to me to find out what I have to say." Most teens will take you through a tunnel of trivia, but continue to listen because they will give you clues as to what the problems actually are. If we don't have time to listen to small problems, we cannot expect the teens to listen to our counsel and guidance. Remember, the *single* greatest compliment you can pay another human being is to *listen* to him.

5) One of the biggest mistakes a counselor can make is to react with shock or disgust. Facial gestures and other body language can give away disappointment or shock. The adolescent is asking for help, not a reprimand. Be sensitive, and try to understand the real problem.

6) Parents, when talking to your kids, sit down in a calm, rational way. Get on their level. Listen for as long as they want to talk. Remember that you represent their greatest hope. Most parents blow up if they find their child has smoked or taken a drink or taken dope or committed an immoral act. They attack the person instead of the problem. Let your child know you are upset because you love him and are concerned about his direction in life. Concern is never out of place.

Think carefully on this: Many times parents are actually upset that they have failed in raising the child. In reality, they are more embarrassed about their failure than they are concerned for the condition of the child. Never turn your back on your child. You are his hope.

7) The unpardonable sin is to betray confidences.

All it takes to ruin your reputation as a counselor is to reveal what was told you in confidence. A parent may do this by bringing up the past when he is upset with his child. Too many preachers are careless in using confidential material as sermon illustrations. As usual, the Scriptures say it best, "Confidence in an unfaithful man in time of trouble is like a broken tooth, and a foot out of joint" (Prov. 25:19).

8) Be positive. A parent, pastor, teacher, or teen who wants to be confided in must be in control of life. If you are always down, always complaining, and if your life is out of control, rest assured no one will seek your help or advice.

9) A good counselor should remind teens that in real life there are no fast solutions. Many teens want instant solutions. This may be the result of seeing every problem, no matter how severe, solved in thirty minutes on television. Most teens I counsel have problems that go back into their past. The three root problems affecting most teens are: 1) moral impurity, which is the result of a poor self-image; 2) bitterness over experiences or treatment they have received in the past; and 3) a temporal value system. They will sacrifice the future for thirty minutes of pleasure or acceptance today.

10) Encourage goal seting. Using John 10:10, explain that God does offer an abundant, exciting life. Help the youth to write out short-term and long-term goals. Point him in the direction to achieve those goals by introducing him to opportunities and resource materials. Set a follow-up time for the next week in which you receive a report.

11) If a counselor is a Christian, he can rely on the Holy Spirit for guidance, help, and strength, and he can use the Bible, the road map to life.

12) Find out what programs are available to help teens—coffee houses, storefronts, hot lines, or successful youth programs at school or church. I use publications and tapes in my counseling. If there is a question you cannot answer, don't be afraid to say, "I don't know." It is no sin to be unable to solve every problem, but it is wrong to talk as an authority about something you know nothing about.

13) Perhaps most important, a counselor must count the cost of counseling *before* he begins. Counseling involves continuity. You may receive phone call after phone call, discouragement after discouragement. Counseling is not a one-time shot, by any means. It may take months for the teen to learn to trust you. In both my wife's case and mine, we did not respond to counseling immediately. There were many trial-and-error mistakes along the way.

My objectives in counseling are three: First, I try to lead the person to a saving knowledge of Jesus Christ. As God, He can create a brand new, exciting life; as Savior, He can forgive sins and failure and take away guilt; as Lord, He cares and understands. "Jesus is the answer" is more than a cliché.

Second, I try to challenge the person to be a victor over life rather than a victim of it, to be part of the solution rather than part of the problem. I try to motivate him to be real, instead of being part of the crowd or an artificial person.

Last, but not least, I try to build bridges between teens and their parents. No young person will ever be happy or fulfilled unless he learns to communicate with his parents. I try to help teens realize that parents have problems and pressures that children have no way of knowing or understanding. If I can help a young person learn to talk and listen to his parents and the heavenly Father, then much of my mission has been accomplished. I truly have been a friend.

What Do You Think?

1. If you desire to help teens in trouble, what is the first attitude you must show them? How do you do this?
2. Which is more important: To listen or to tell all the information you know? Why is listening so important?
3. Is caring enough? What about knowing how to help? What tools can you give a person to help them help themselves by changing their attitudes?
4. Practice encouraging goal setting by first making out a goal sheet of your own. Use short-term and long-term goals and be prepared to share these as examples in helping others.
5. Does everyone who comes to you really want help? How can you determine whether they really want to change?
6. Can a teen-ager succeed in life if he does well in school, has friends, is a Christian and happy in his church, but does not have a good relationship with his parents? How can you help others with this problem?

12.

The Way of Escape

THE CONTEMPORARY DRUG SCENE presents a paradox: Those who are weekend users are doing all they can to get into the scene, while those in the scene would like to be out. Obviously, this is the age of disillusionment. Everyone wants to be happy; everyone is searching for peace. No matter what part of the world you travel, you will find people caught up in this relentless search.

Teens don't need to be told that they never should have started on the road to drug abuse. I do not put them down, for I myself tried to find life in a bottle, a needle, a pill. I did everything to find love and peace and joy. No matter how popular I was, or who I was dating, or how high I got, or how much money I had, I still knew there was more to life. I was tired of being part of a crowd going nowhere. I was tired of traveling dead-end streets. And then, I met Someone who really cared about me.

This last chapter is what I tell young people whom I counsel. You will note that I am speaking directly to them. I would hope that you, the reader, will share this with someone needing help.

No doubt, some of you reading this are heavily into drugs and want out. Some of you are tired of doing what the crowd wants you to do. Many of you feel life is hopeless, that no one cares, that there is no cure. It is true, medical science has failed to find the answer; methadone centers reduce drug-related thefts but offer no real solution to addiction. The Federal Narcotic Hospital in Lexington, Kentucky, was built to help addicts escape from the drug trap. The government spent millions of dollars to build, equip, and maintain this hospital. The per patient cost ran into thousands of dollars. Staffed with competent psychologists, doctors, and nurses who used the most modern technology and medicines known, the hospital reported only a 2 percent cure rate for addicts. Imagine—only 2 percent were able to escape. The results were so discouraging that the facility was closed.

But there *is* hope! The Pulpit in the Shadows of Houston, Texas, reported a documented 80 percent permanent cure rate. David Wilkerson, author of *The Cross and the Switchblade*, reports an 80 percent cure rate of hard-core junkies in his organization. Drug Addicts Rehabilitation Enterprises (D.A.R.E.) in Albuquerque, New Mexico, reports a 73 percent recovery rate. How do these centers have such success rates with this dreaded problem when other approaches fail? The answer is simple. They offer no crutch, no medication of any kind; all they offer is the Bible.

Freddie Gage, of the Pulpit in the Shadows, said, "We don't try to get kids to kick dope. Rather, we offer the doper something he has searched for all along, something he was created to have and will search for until he finds it or dies, whichever comes first. We offer him a personal relationship with God through His Son, Jesus Christ, that can meet every need in his life, even the very needs that caused him to turn to drugs in the first place."[1] Yes, the supernatural power of God the Creator can set the captured free.

How does one go about receiving the new life? Here are four things you must realize:

1) *It's natural to be turned off.* The reason you are restless, bored, and confused is because you are a sinner! Now, you already knew that, but there is more to it. Sin makes you a loser and will eventually destroy you. You are incomplete, and the reason you live like you do is that you are trying to fill that void in your life. The Bible teaches that no matter how hard man tries to fill that void, he will fail. Sin will rob and ruin him. "For all have sinned, and come short of the glory of God" (Rom. 3:23). "The wages of sin is death...." (Rom. 6:23). This sin reveals itself either in active rebellion or in passive indifference.

2) *But God loves you in spite of the fact that you have sinned.* You are important to God. He loves you very much. We know this because: You were created by God out of love (Gen. 1:26); God loved you so much He sent Jesus to die for you (John 3:16); He cares for you right now (1 Pet. 5:7).

3) *Only the Creator can give you real life.* The real life is exciting; Jesus came to give life in all of its fullness (John 10:10). It is everlasting. "...Whosoever believeth in him should not perish, but have everlasting life" (John 3:16).

4) *You can be unhooked forever.* God is "...not willing that any should perish, but that all should come to repentance" (2 Pet. 3:9). "But God commendeth his love toward us, in that, while we were yet sinners, Christ died for us" (Rom. 5:8). "Greater love hath no man than this, that a man lay down his life for his

friends" (John 15:13). By His death on the cross, our sins have already been paid for and can be forgiven. Because of His resurrection, He is alive to give you new life. To be unhooked means the same as the Bible word "repentance." It means to have a change of mind.

Now, when you make connection with Jesus Christ, you must open your heart and life and invite this living Savior to come in, to forgive your past, and to take control of your future. He is the cure for drug addiction and alcoholism. It doesn't matter how long a person has been addicted—he or she can be cured. Here are five steps to meet the Cure, Jesus Christ:

1) *Admit you are hooked!* It doesn't matter whether you take off (fix) once a day or ten times a day; you are hooked. So why not admit it? Quit talking about a big habit or a little habit. A habit is a habit. You are hooked or you aren't; you are an alcoholic or you aren't. So be honest. Don't let a habit grow worse while you are deciding.

Quit trying to cut down on your habit. You can't do it. You know you can't help yourself, so why continue to try? No one can help you if you just want to control your habit or be a weekend user. There is no such thing as a controlled habit. You will shoot all the dope you can get, and you know it! You will drink all the booze you can get your hands on. Admit to yourself, "I am a drug addict; I am hooked." Or, "I am an alcoholic. I can't help myself." Then you are ready for the next step.

2) *Quit looking for an easy way out!* There is no simple, magic cure. There are no synthetic drugs or substances that can cure you. Hospitals can't help you on a permanent basis. Just ask anyone who has

been there. As soon as you're out of the hospital, you're back to the habit. You can go back to the hospital one hundred times, see a hundred psychiatrists, but you will still be the same—hooked! A clinic can't help you either, and deep in your heart you know it. Maybe you won't admit it, but it's true. How many times have you tried a clinic already?

No doctor, psychiatrist, or hypnotist can cure you. A doctor can pacify you with some pills. A psychiatrist can tell you why you're an addict, but he can't cure you. Posthypnotic suggestion can't combat a strung-out habit. Seminars and group therapy programs do not produce permanent cures, in spite of all the claims. Homes that practice seminar sessions for addicts cannot put into you what it takes to stay clean when you are on your own and in a real crisis.

Cold turkey is the best and quickest way to start a cure. Throwing away the bottle is the only way to stop drinking. It's the best way.

Don't ask for help just to please someone else. You are only fooling yourself if you look for help just to keep a wife, mother, or friend happy. You have to want to help yourself.

You are going to be sick, but you're not a little baby. You were big enough to get into this; you're big enough to get out.

3) *Give yourself to God!* He is the only one who can cure you. Nothing is impossible with Him! You must believe that the Bible is the word of God. "Ye shall know the truth, and the truth shall make you free" (John 8:32). It is not enough just to believe in God. You must believe in His Son, Jesus Christ, as well. The Bible makes this promise to you: If you will confess Him as your Savior, He will make you into a

new man. The old life will pass away, and everything will become new. You will become a new creature (2 Cor. 5:17).

Open up your heart to God, even more than you would to a psychiatrist, and tell Him all about your problems. Then confess to Jesus all your sins and every bad thing that you can remember you have done. Ask Him to forgive your sins and to come into your heart. He will help drive out the desire for drugs and give you power over it! Don't just think prayers to God—talk out loud to Him. He understands you and knows all about your sins and problems, but He wants you to talk to Him. While you are talking out loud to God, you will suddenly know what prayer really is.

Read the Bible everyday, and fill your mind from its verses. Keep asking for His help, even if you have to do it a thousand times a day. He will never get tired of listening.

You must have faith in God! When you connect with a pusher, you don't really know what you are getting. You shoot or snort the substance without testing it under a microscope, because you have faith it is junk. If you can trust a dope pusher, why can't you trust God? He never lets you down.

4) *Start planning your life all over again!* The moment you surrender your life to God is the time to start planning all over again. Think back to the time before you started using drugs or drinking alcohol. What was your ambition? Find what you want to do and then start making plans.

All your plans must start with God. Make Him your partner. Give God first chance to use your life. It may be He will want you to help other addicts when you are fully cured.

You can never be around your old neighborhood or your old friends. Stay away from your old life as if it were hell itself. Stay away from your old hangouts instead of testing yourself to see if you are cured—that would be tempting God. Find new friends and brothers who are clean.

If you have no plans for your life and you are sure you can't help others, then mark down on a piece of paper five things you think you would like to do or be. Spend a few weeks investigating these five things. Pray about them. Then choose the one that appeals to you most. You must have a goal. You can never again be a loafer. You can never again be a floater without ambition. Know what you want to do and then go after it. Indecision will ruin you.

You will learn to love the things you once hated and hate the things you once loved. You can do the right things now, because God gives you the power to do them.

5) *Shake off all your old fears!* Fear is the demon that turned you into a drug addict to begin with. When you turn your life over to God, you never have to fear again. When Jesus comes to live in your heart, He drives away all fears and doubts.

Don't be afraid you will go back to the needle or to the bottle or to any artificial high. God guarantees a 100 percent cure. As long as you stay with God, He will stay with you. If you forsake God, you will go back to being an addict or an alcoholic. I saw a poster once that said, "If you don't feel close to God, guess who moved!" God remains the same. When Jesus comes to be with you, you need never fear.

Don't be afraid of your past. When God forgives your sins, He forgets them. He will not hold them against you. Make restitution when you can, but when you can't, leave it in God's hands. Don't ever be afraid God will drop you. He has never done that, and He even promises to send angels to watch over you in all your ways.

Don't ever be afraid of what people will say or think. Keep your eyes on Jesus, and you will never be disappointed or confused.

When fear starts coming into your mind to confuse and bother you, when you start getting restless, get away by yourself and kneel before God. Ask Him to keep you in perfect peace. He will keep you from all your fears.

Now that Christ lives in you, begin your new life by letting *Christ turn you on* . . .

. . . to pardon for past mistakes:

"Seek ye the Lord while he may be found, call ye upon him while he is near: Let the wicked forsake his way, and the unrighteous man his thoughts: and let him return unto the Lord, and he will have mercy upon him; and to our God, for he will abundantly pardon" (Isa. 55:6, 7).

"I will cleanse them from all their iniquity [wickedness], whereby they have sinned against me; and I will pardon all their iniquities . . ." (Jer. 33:8).

"If we confess [agree with God] our sins, he is faithful and just to forgive us our sins, and to cleanse us from all unrighteousness" (1 John 1:9).

There was once a convicted murderer who received a government pardon from execution. However, he rejected the pardon and requested death instead. Could a man reject a pardon? The legal decision: A pardon is only valid when it is received. The man was executed, according to his choice.

... *to peace* (mental calm, mental tranquility, mental security, victory over the battle for the mind):

"Peace I leave with you, my peace I give unto you: not as the world giveth, give I unto you. Let not your heart be troubled, neither let it be afraid" (John 14:27).

"Let the peace of God rule in your hearts..." (Col. 3:15).

"For he is our peace..." (Eph. 2:14).

"And the peace of God, which passeth all understanding, shall keep your hearts and minds through Christ Jesus" (Phil. 4:7).

What wonderful hope this is in the age of anxiety, fear, and uncertainty!

... *to power* (literally means "to be able"—hence Jesus will give you the power to live a life worth living, the ability to live a life pleasing to God):

"I can do all things through Christ which strengtheneth me" (Phil. 4:13).

"In all these things we are more than conquerors through him that loved us" (Rom. 8:37).

"For God hath not given us the spirit of fear; but of power, and of love, and of a sound mind" (2 Tim. 1:7).

Jesus gives you the power to be your own person. You don't have to be part of the herd. Don't fly in a flock like a duck or goose when Jesus gives you the power to soar like an eagle. Without Jesus, you are like a beautiful car with an empty gas tank.

... *to purpose* (a direction, a goal, an aim). You don't have to be bored, empty and restless. You don't have to wander aimlessly like a ship without a rudder:

"...I am come that they might have life, and that they might have it more abundantly" (John 10:10).

Pascal, the physicist and philosopher, said, "There is a God-shaped vacuum in the heart of every man which cannot be satisfied by any created thing but by God, the Creator, who is made known through Jesus Christ."

Augustine said, "Our hearts are restless, O God, until we have rest in thee."

The day your new life begins is your spiritual birthday. It is only the beginning of a wonderful life in which you will grow and learn each and every day.

Jesus said, "...I am the way, the truth, and the life: no man cometh unto the Father, but by me" (John 14:6).

What Do You Think?

1. Write down John 3:16. Now, using that verse and others you know, describe what it means to be born again.
2. Does God ever stop loving a person? Do you think there are sins God cannot forgive?
3. Once a person is born again, will he ever be tempted to use drugs or sin again? How can he fight this?
4. If you are to have peace with God, what is your part in the relationship? What is God's part and how does He fulfill it?
5. GRACE has been described as God's Riches At Christ's Expense. Can you describe what it means to you to have faith in God? Give an example of complete trust.

6. Read Hebrews Chapter 11 in the Bible. This is called the "Faith Chapter." Think of the problems you and others face. Now compare these to the problems overcome by faith in Hebrews Chapter 11. Is there anything too hard for God?

Glossary

A's—AMPHETAMINES—Uppers, speed.

ACAPULCO GOLD—A supposedly superior grade of marijuana which is gold in color and grown in the vicinity of Acapulco, Mexico.

ACID—LSD (lysergic acid diethylamide).

ACID HEAD—A frequent user of LSD.

ADDICT—Person with physical dependence on a drug.

AMPED—"Wired" on methedrine or crystal.

ANGEL DUST—PCP, an animal tranquilizer, an hallucinogen.

ARE YOU HOLDING?—Do you have any dope?

BABY—One who has a small heroin habit, who is just getting started.

BACK TRACK—To allow blood to come back into the syringe during an intravenous injection.

BAD SCENE—Uncomfortable or unfriendly surroundings, a bad situation.

BAG—Packet of drugs; for example, a bag of marijuana or ten to twenty-five dollars' worth of heroin; also the category into which one fits.

BALLOON—A bag of heroin sold in a rubber balloon.

BANG—An injection of drugs.

BARB—Barbiturates.

BENNIES—Benzedrine, an amphetamine.

BENT—An above-average high.

BERNICE—Cocaine.

BERNIE'S FLAKE—Cocaine.

BIG C—Cocaine.

BIG D—LSD.

BUNDLE—A packet of drugs.

BLACK BEAUTIES—Amphetamines.

BLANK—Extremely low-grade narcotics (trash).

BLAST—Strong effect from a drug.

BLOW A JOINT—To smoke a marijuana cigarette.

BLOW CHARLIE OR SNOW—To sniff cocaine.

BLOW HORSE—To sniff heroin.

BLOW A MIND—To escape from personal reality.

BLOW IT—To bungle a situation; lose control; become very angry; lose your cool; lose face.

BLUE ANGES—Amytal, a barbiturate (amobarbital sodium).

BLUE BIRDS—Amytal.

BLUE DEVILS—Amytal.

BLUE HEAVEN—Amytal.

BLUE VELVET—Paregoric (camphorated tincture of opium)/pyribenzamine (an antihistamine) mixed injection.

BOGART—To monopolize; to fail to pass a joint.

BOMBITA—Injection of amphetamine (crystals, speed, etc.) sometimes taken with heroin.

BONG-SNAKE—Dope in a water pipe.

BOOT—To allow blood to flow back and forth into the syringe during the injection of drugs.

BOWL—The amount of pot or hash that fits in the bowl of a pipe.

BREAD—Money.

BREW—Beer.

BRICK—Two and one-half pounds of drug—the size of a shoe box—also called a "kilo."

BROCCOLI—Marijuana.

BROWN—Heroin from Mexico, usually light brown in color.

BUM TRIP—A bad experience with psychedelics; a drug experience with little effect.

BUMMER—A bad experience with psychedelics; or any bad experience with the law, school, or parents.

BURN—To sell some other substance, such as sugar, for dope; very bad dope.

BURN OUT—To use so much dope it destroys the mind; a sclerotic blood vessel caused by too many injections; someone who has "burned out"; also, someone who has outgrown or matured out of his habit.

BUSTED—Arrested in drug-related crime (pushing, selling, possession).

BUTTONS—The sections of the peyote cactus.

C—Cocaine.

CADET—New addict.

CAN—About one ounce of marijuana; the quantity that can be carried in a Prince Albert tobacco can.

CANDY—Barbiturates; any drug one prefers.

CAP—Capsule of drugs; gelatin capsule used to package drugs; a packet of heroin.

CAT—Any male.

CATCH UP—Withdrawal process.

CECIL—Cocaine.

CHARLIE—Cocaine.

CHASING THE BAG—Shopping around to find the best quality of street heroin.

CHICK—Any female; cocaine.

CHIPPING—Taking narcotics occasionally.

CHRISTMAS TREES—Tuinal (secobarbital/ambarbital); Dexamyl capsules.

CLEAN—To quit drugs completely.

COASTING—Under the influence of drugs.

COAST-TO-COAST—Long-lasting amphetamine capsules.

COKE—Cocaine.

COKIE—A cocaine addict.

COLD TURKEY—Coming down from heroin without medication (refers to the goose-flesh appearance of skin).

COMING DOWN—The end of a drug experience; recovering from a trip.

CONNECTION—Drug supplier; pusher.

CONTACT HIGH—Psychological feeling of being high merely from being around a person who is high, usually on psychedelics, speed, or marijuana.

COOKIN'—To have a really good time.

COOK UP—To heat a drug prior to injection.

COP—To get anything; to get a drug (usually heroin).

CO-PILOTS—Long-lasting amphetamine capsules.

COP-OUT—To succumb to the establishment; to lose one's cool; also, to inform the police.

CRANK—Methamphetamine in powdered form.

CRASH—Coming down; to sleep; to pass out from drugs; also, to spend the night.

CRASH PAD—Place where drug users end trips or withdraw from amphetamines.

CRYSTAL—Methamphetamine.

CUBE HEAD—A frequent user of LSD.

CUBE—LSD.

CUT—To dilute drugs by adding milk sugar or another inert substance.

DEALER—Drug supplier.

DECK—A packet of narcotics, usually heroin.

DEXIES—Dexedrine, Dexamyl.

DIME—Ten dollars.

DIME BAG—Ten dollars' worth of narcotics.

DIRTY—Possessing drugs; using drugs, especially heroin.

DOLLIES—Dolophine (aslo known as methadone, a synthetic narcotic).

DOPER—A frequent user of drugs.

DOWNERS—Barbiturates (sedatives, alcohol, tranquilizers, depressants).

DROP—To take pills or capsules by mouth (to swallow).

DRY UP—To stop using for a while; also, to dry out.

DUBIE—A joint, a marijuana cigarette.

DUDE—A male.

DUMMY—A purchase which does not contain narcotics.

DUSTER—A heroin cigarette.

DYNAMITE—High-quality drugs, usually heroin.

EYE OPENERS—Amphetamines.

FINK—To inform on someone; to betray.

FIX—An injection of narcotics.

FLAKE—Cocaine.

FLASH—A strong, pleasurable sensation; also, a sudden realization.

FLASH BACK—A recurring LSD trip.

FLIP OUT—To lose control because of a hallucinogen.

FLOW—"Don't fight it"; "flow with"; the effect of a drug.

FLOATING—Under the influence of drugs.

FOOTBALLS—A combination of destriamphetamine/amphetamine.

FOXY—Looking good (especially a female).

FREAK—Drug user, i.e., bottle freak, needle user.

FREAK OUT—A bad trip with drugs; to be unable to cope with the immediate situation; to become hysterical (to flip out).

FREEBASING—The smoking of cocaine paste in a water pipe.

FREEBIE—Something for nothing; free.

FUNKY—Dirty, low-down, earthy; also refers to types of music.

FUZZ—The police.

GAGE—Marijuana.

GEE HEAD—Paregoric user.

GET A HIT—To inject drugs intravenously.

GET OFF—To take any drug; also, to feel the effects of a drug; to begin the drug trip or experience.

GLAD RAG—The cloth or handkerchief that is saturated with a material to be inhaled.

GOOD TRIP—A happy experience with psychedelics.

GOOF BALLS—Barbiturates, usually sleeping pills.

GOOFING—To be under the influence of a barbiturate; to hang out.

GORILLA, KING KONG, MIGHTY JOE YOUNG—Large heroin habit.

GRASS—Marijuana.

GREENIES—Amphetamines.

G—The morphine obtained from boiling down paregoric.

GUIDE—Anyone not on drugs who babysits with another under the influence.

H—Heroin.

HABIT—Addiction to drugs.

HANG UP—A personal problem about a particular subject.

HARD NARCOTICS—Opiates such as heroin and morphine.

HARD STUFF—Heroin or morphine.

HASH—Hashish, the resin of cannabis.

HAWK—LSD.

HAY—Marijuana.

HEAD—Someone who uses drugs, or any particular drug (such as "cube head" for LSD).

HEARTS—Dexedrine tablets (amphetamines), named because of the shape.

HEAT—The police.

HEAVENLY BLUES—A type of morning glory seed and LSD.

HEAVY—An altered state of consciousness, usually pleasant; important or serious; a strong dose of a drug.

HIGH—To be under the influence of drugs.

HIT—A shot of dope; a puff; a snort of anything.

HOLDING—Having drugs in one's possession.

HOOKED—Addicted or dependent on drugs such as heroin.

HOP HEAD—A narcotics addict.

HORROR DRUG—Belladonna preparation.

HORSE—Heroin.

HUSTLE—A nonviolent but illegal means of making money other than a straight job (dealing, prostitution, etc.).

HUSTLER—Prostitute.

HYPE—A narcotics addict, usually on the needle.

INSTANT ZEN—LSD.

JIVE—Dishonest, untrustworthy.

JOINT—A marijuana cigarette.

JOLLY BEANS—Pep pills.

JOY POPPER—An irregular user of narcotics.

JUNK—Heroin.

JUNKIE—An addict.

KICK THE HABIT—To stop using drugs (so-called from the fact that during withdrawal the leg muscles twitch).

KILLER—Really good.

KILO—A kilogram, or two-and-one-half pounds of anything, usually marijuana; nicknamed "kee."

KONG KONG—Two-hundred-dollar- (or more) a-day heroin habit.

L.A. TURNABOUTS—Long-lasting amphetamine capsules.

LAME—A self-imposed adjective for drug addicts; to be stupid, foolish, unhip.

LAY OUT—Equipment for injecting drugs (spoon, needle, matches, syringe), also called a "set of works"; opium smoker's outfit.

LAY UP—To stay off the streets once a large supply of heroin has been obtained.

LEMONADE—Poor quality heroin.

LID—One ounce of marijuana.

LINE—A dosage of cocaine; a hit; a shot; a snort of cocaine.

LIPTON TEA—Poor-quality heroin.

LOADED—Very stoned; drunk; also, sick.

LOCO WEED—Marijuana.

LSD—Lysergic acid diethylamide; a powerful hallucinogen.

M—Morphine.

MAINLINE—To inject drugs into a vein.

MAKE IT—To make love; to go somewhere.

THE MAN—Police; also, someone to buy drugs from.

MANICURE—To remove dirt, seeds, and stems from marijuana.

MARY JANE—Marijuana.
MELLOW—Happy, relaxed.
MESC—Mescaline.
METH—Methamphetamine in liquid or crystal form.
MIKES—Micrograms (millionths of a gram).
MISS—When the tip of the needle slips out of the vein or goes through the vein and the drug is injected into the surrounding tissue.
MISS EMMA—Morphine.
MDA—Hallucinogen.
MMDA—Hallucinogen.
MONKEY—Morphine; a small heroin habit.
MONKEY ON BACK—Any drug addiction that must be fed, especially addiction to heroin.
MUSHROOMS—Psilocybin.
MUNCHIES—The overwhelming desire for somthing to eat, usually after smoking marijuana.
NARC—Narcotics agent, undercover cop.
NEEDLE FREAK—Someone who enjoys injecting almost anything; to get a sexual flash from the injection.
NEMBY—Pentobarbital sodium.
NICKEL—Five dollars (as in a "nickel bag," meaning five dollars' worth of a drug).
NOD—To get sleepy from heroin or other depressants.
O.D.—An overdose of drugs; too much; a fatal dose.
OFF—Stoned.
ON THE NOD—Sleepy from narcotics.
ON TOP OF IT—In control of a situation.
OUTFIT—Drug injection kit (eyedropper, pacifier, or syringe, and needle).
OUT OF SIGHT—Usually, a very pleasurable situation.
P—Peyote.
PACK—A packet of drugs.
PAD—House or apartment; place where one lives.
PANIC—A critical shortage of drugs in the streets.
PAPER—A small packet of dope; a prescription; a bad check.
PCP—Phencyclidine, a hallucinogen.
PEANUT BUTTER—Heroin.
PEARLY GATES—LSD; morning glory seeds.
PEP PILL—Amphetamines.
PEOPLE—One's friends or connection.

PIG—Policeman.

PILLHEAD—A habitual user of barbiturates or amphetamines.

PIPE—Large vein.

POP—To inject drugs; swallow a pill.

POT HEAD—A heavy marijuana user.

POT—Marijuana.

PURPLE HEART—Dexamyl; combination of dexedrine and aanrytal (name taken from the shape and color).

PUSHER—Drug dealer.

RAP—To talk with (from "rapport").

RAINBOWS—Tuinal (amobarbital and secobarbital), a barbiturate combination in blue and red capsules.

RED DEVILS, REDS, RED BIRDS, ETC.—Seconal, a barbiturate.

REEFER—A partially smoked marijuana cigarette.

REENTRY—The return from a trip.

RIG—Paraphernalia for injection.

RIP OFF—Steal.

RIPPED—Extremely stoned.

ROACH—The butt, or last part, of a marijuana cigarette.

ROACH CLIP—Clip used to hold butt of a joint.

RUN—An amphetamine binge.

RUNNER—One who delivers drugs and makes connections for purchase.

RUSH—A strong, pleasurable feeling following the taking of a drug.

SACRED MUSHROOMS—Psilocybin.

SATCH COTTON—Cotton used to strain drugs before injection; may be used again if supplies are gone.

SCAG—Heroin.

SCORE—To obtain anything, usually drugs or sex; to purchase drugs.

SET UP—To arrange for a person to be arrested by planting dope on him or by having the police buy dope from him.

SHOOT UP—To inject drugs just under the skin.

SHOOTING GALLERY—A place where people go to shoot drugs when they have no other place to go; a communal drug hangout.

SKIN POP—To inject drugs just under the skin.

SLAMMER—A jail or prison.

SLEEPERS—Downers; barbiturates; central nervous system depressants.

SMACK—Heroin.

SMOKE—Wood alcohol.

SNORT, SNIFF—To sniff or inhale drugs (usually cocaine, heroin, speed, or smoke from a roach) through the mucous membranes of the nose.

SNOW—Cocaine or heroin.

SPACED OUT—Out of touch; not all there; usually the result of prolonged use of strong drugs.

SPEED—Amphetamine or methamphetamine, powerful central nervous system stimulants.

SPEEDBALL—Cocaine and heroin; percodan and methedrine.

SPEEDING—Under the influence of speed.

SPEED FREAK—One who takes a lot of speed.

SPIKE—Hypodermic needle.

SPOON—About one gram of drugs.

STASH—A supply of drugs stored in a secure place.

STEAMBOAT—A device for smoking marijuana or hashish.

STEPPED ON—When a drug is repeatedly cut with cheaper substances to increase profits; primarily with cocaine.

STICK—A marijuana cigarette.

STONED—To be high on drugs; an altered state of consciousness.

STOOLIE—An informer.

STP—An hallucinogen; Serenity, Tranquility, and Peace; DOM.

STRAIGHT—Someone who does not use drugs.

STRUNG OUT—Addicted for a long time; in bad shape.

SUGAR—LSD or heroin.

SUPERWEED—Pot or parsley treated with PCP.

SYNDICATE ACID—PCP.

TAB—A tablet; capsules containing LSD-25.

TAKE OFF—To rob; to get high; to inject heroin.

TEA—Marijuana.

TIE OFF—To apply pressure on the vein so it will stand out, making the injection easier.

TOGETHER—In control of oneself; composed.

TOKE—One puff on a joint.

TRACKS—Scars on the arms and body from injections; needle holes.

TRICK—Something done to make money; act of prostitution.

TRIP—An experience on a drug, usually an hallucinogen.

TRIPPING OUT—High on hallucinogens.

TRUCK DRIVERS—Amphetamines.

TRUCKIN' (Keep on)—To keep on going with self-confidence.

TURN ON—To take a drug; to give someone else a drug.

TURKEY TROTS—Marks and scars from hypodermic needles.

TWENTY-FIVE—LSD.

UP FRONT—Honest, candid, blunt.

UPPERS—Stimulants; amphetamines.

UNDERGROUND—The drug subculture.

WAKE UP—The first shot of heroin or amphetamine of the day.

WASTED—Extremely stoned; also, hurt, injured or sick; malnourished because of an extended speed run; killed.

WEED—Marijuana.

WHITE LADY—Heroin.

WINGS—The first mainline injection of drugs.

WIPED OUT—See WASTED.

WIRED—Addicted.

WORKS—Equipment for injecting drugs.

WITHDRAWAL—The symptoms of sickness that accompany abrupt disuse of a drug that is physically addicting.

YELLOW JACKETS—Nembutal sodium capsules.

YEN—Dope craving after one has been clean for a while.

YEN SLEEP—A drowsy, restless state during the withdrawal period.

ZAP—To put someone or something down; to shoot someone.

ZEN—LSD.

ZONKED OUT—Really loaded; overdosed.

Notes

CHAPTER 1

[1]Dr. Clyde M. Narramore, *Counseling Youth* (Grand Rapids: Zondervan, 1966), p. 38.

[2]David Augsburger, *So What? Everybody's Doing It!* (Chicago: Moody Press, 1969), pp. 18, 19.

[3]Carlton Turner, Ph.D., "Drugs and Kids—How to Keep Them Apart," *Health Spectrum*, (Fall/1983 Winter/1984) p. 11.

[4]"Teens' Cigarette, Alcohol Use May Foreshadow Drug Abuse," *The Atlanta Constitution*, July 18, 1984, p. 6A.

[5]"Beached Whales," *Science Digest*, December, 1976, p. 22.

[6]"Locusts: Teeth of the Wind," *National Geographic*, August, 1969, pp. 200–213.

[7]Frank Cortina, *Stroke a Slain Warrior* (New York: Columbia University Press, 1971), p. 1.

[8]"Twelve Things You Should Know About Marijuana," *Consumers' Research*, April 1980.

[9]*High Times*, August 1984, pp. 28, 29, 95.

[10]Proverbs 9:17, 18, King James Version.

[11]Billy Graham, *World Aflame* (Garden City, New York: Doubleday and Company, 1965), p. 48.

CHAPTER 2

[1]Freddie Gage, *Everything You Always Wanted To Know About Dope* (Houston: Pulpit Productions, 1971), p. 22.

[2]Alfred Jay Bollet, M.D., "Drug Abuse: An Important Issue," *Medical Times Journal*, October 1983, pp. 17, 25.

[3]"Twleve Things You Should Know," *Consumer's Research*, April 1980, p.8.

[4]West, L. J.; Maxwell, D. S.; Noble, E. P.; and Solomon, D. H., *Annals of Internal Medicine*, 100 (3): 405–416, 1984.

[5]"Alcohol's Effect on Sexual Perfomance," *Observer News* from the Johnson Institute, Vol. 6, No. 2, June 1984, p. 5.

[6]National Clearinghouse for Alcohol Information, 1981 Fact Sheet.

[7]R. M. Bennett et al., "Alcohol and Human Physical Aggression," *Quarterly Journal Studies Alcohol* (30:870, 1969).

Notes

[8]D. W. Goodwin, "Alcohol in Suicide and Homicide," *Quarterly Journal Studies Alcohol* (34:144, 1973).

[9]Sidney Cohen, *The Drug Dilemma*, 2nd ed. (New York: McGraw-Hill, 1976), p. 59.

[10]The Johnson Institute, 1977.

[11]*Observer News*, p. 8.

[12]*Observer News*, p. 5.

[13]Ross J. McLennan, *Booze, Bucks, Bamboozle and You!* (Oklahoma City: Sane Press, 1978), p. 6.

[14]J. R. DeFoe, W. Breed, L.A. Breed, "Drinking on Television: A Five-Year Study," *Journal of Drug Education*, (13 [1]: 25-38, 1983).

[15]1984 Statistical Analysis, United States Department of Commerce, 1984.

CHAPTER 3

[1]National Institute of Drug Abuse, 1982.

[2]"Crashing on Cocaine," *Time*, April 11, 1983, p. 25.

[3]Joseph A. Pursch, M.D., *Alcoholism*, (September/October 1983).

[4]Gabriel G. Nahas, M.D., Ph.D., "Cocaine, The Great Addicter," October 1980.

[5]Laurence Gonzales, "Cocaine—A Special Report," September 1984.

CHAPTER 4

[1]Sidney Cohen, M.D., *The Beyond Within: The LSD Story* (New York: Atheneum, 1965), pp. 26-31.

[2]Robert S. DeKopp, *The Master Game* (New York: Dell Publishing Company, 1968), p. 48.

[3]Ibid.

[4]Jim Tuell, *The Drug Scene* (Dallas: Tane Press, 1972).

[5]Nancy Gray, *Chemical Use/Abuse and The Female Reproductive System*, 2nd ed. (Phoenix: Do It Now Foundation, 1976), p. 11.

CHAPTER 7

[1]*The Observer*, p. 4.

[2]Dennis D. Nelson, "Frequently Seen Stages in Adolescent Chemical Use," CompCare Publications, Minneapolis, Minnesota, 1978.

CHAPTER 8

[1]*The Observer*, p. 1.

[2]R. E. Clark and D. Duckworth, "The Influence of Information Sources and Grade Level on the Diffusion and Adoption of Marijuana," *The Journal of Drug Issues*, 5 (2), 1975, pp. 177-188.

[3]George A. Buttrick, *Christ and Man's Dilemma*, (Nashville: Abingdon-Cokesbury Press, 1946).

[4]John Ruskin, *Sesame and Lilies* (1865), quoted from *World Treasury of Religious Quotations*, ed. R. Woods (Westminster, Md.: Christian Classics, 1966).

[5]Quoted from the Chicago Sun Times, copyright 1978.

[6]Karl Menninger, *The Vital Balance: The Life Process in Mental Health and Illness* (New York: Viking Press, 1963).

[7]C. S. Lovett, *What's a Parent to Do?* (Baldwin Park, Calif.: Personal Christianity, 1971).

CHAPTER 9
[1]Charles H. Spurgeon, *Lectures To My Students*, new ed. (Grand Rapids: Zondervan, 1955), pp. 9, 10.
[2]Aelred Graham, *Christian Thought and Action*, quoted from *World Treasury of Religious Quotations*, ed. R. Woods (Westminster, Md.: Christian Classics, 1966).

CHAPTER 10
[1]"President Decries Violence in Classrooms," Associated Press wire service, *Fort Myers News Press*, January 9, 1984.
[2]Cohen, *The Drug Dilemma.*
[3]Boris Sokoloff, *The Permissive Society* (New Rochelle, N.Y.: Arlington House, 1971).
[4]"Thoughts of a Drop Out," *Today's Education* (Feb., 1970).
[5]Cohen, *The Drug Dilemma*, p. 120.
[6]Sylvia Ashton-Warner, *Spearpoint: "Teacher" in America* (New York: Alfred A. Knopf, Inc., 1972).

CHAPTER 12
[1]Freddie Gage, *Pulpit in the Shadows* (Houston: Pulpit Productions, 1970), pp. 120–123.